The Three Vehicles of
Buddhist Practice

The Three Vehicles of Buddhist Practice

by

Khenchen Thrangu, Rinpoche
Geshe Lharampa

Translated by
Ken Holmes

Edited by
Clark Johnson, Ph. D.

Copyright © 1998 by Khenchen Thrangu
All rights reserved. No part of this book, either text or art, may be reproduced in any form, electronic or otherwise, without written permission from the Namo Buddha Publications.

Published by
Namo Buddha Seminar
1390 Kalmia Avenue
Boulder, CO 80304-1813 USA
Tel. : (303) 449-6608
Fax: (303) 440-0882
E-mail: cjohnson@ix.netcom.com

These teachings were given at Samye Ling, Scotland in 1984.

May all beings have happiness and the cause of happiness;
May they all be free from sorrow and the cause of sorrow;
May they never be separated from the bliss that is without sorrow;
May they live in equanimity, free from attachment and aversion.

Table of Contents

Foreword	9
1. The Hīnayāna Path	13
The four noble truths	15
The belief in a self	23
The five paths	25
Meditation on the Hīnayāna path	30
The Practice on the Hīnayāna Path	40
2. The Mahāyāna Path	47
The four immeasurables	48
Interdependent origination	53
Relative and absolute truth	56
Buddha-nature	60
The six pāramitās	64
3. The Vajrayāna Path	73
The importance of the guru	76
Meditation on the yidams	78
The completion stage	84
Meditating directly on mind	85
Insight meditation	96
Notes	109
The Glossary of Terms	111
Glossary of Tibetan Terms	119
Bibliography	121
About the Author	123
Index	125

Acknowledgements

We would like to thank the many persons who helped make this book possible. First of all, we would like to thank Ken Holmes for translating this work. We would also like to thank Gaby Hollmann for transcribing the tapes and Jean Johnson and Dr. Alta Brown for editing the manuscript.

Finally, we would like to thank Debra Calloway and Eric and Patricia Wilson who made the printing of this book possible.

We would like to thank Benjamin Jobe for his photograph of KTD in Woodstock, NY and his photograph of Thrangu Rinpoche on the cover.

Foreword

The Venerable Thrangu Rinpoche has been recognized as an outstanding teacher by His Holiness the Dalai Lama who gave him his Geshe degree in the early 1960's. He was then asked to establish the Buddhist curriculum for the Shedra at Rumtek Monastery by His Holiness the Gyalwa Karmapa. There he spent almost two decades teaching Tibetan Buddhism to the lamas of the Kagyu lineage.

In 1969 Thrangu Rinpoche was invited to the West and began a series of yearly visits to Samye Ling in Scotland where he shared his vast knowledge with Western students. He first taught the *Uttara Tantra* and the *Jewel Ornament of Liberation.* Interspersed with commentaries on these great works, he gave teachings on dharma topics for Western students. This book on the *Three Vehicles of Buddhist Practice* or *The Three Yānas* was part of these teachings.

The Three Vehicles of Buddhist Practice takes the reader through the levels of practice—all of which are essential to master if one is to achieve enlightenment. The hīnayāna level of teachings explain in detail the four noble truths and the meditational methods of this level. Thrangu Rinpoche also tells his students when discussing the hīnayāna that they should not in any way consider this a lower or inferior path. Rather it is more like the lower rungs in a ladder, you cannot reach the top without using them. Rinpoche then describes the path of the bodhisattva—that Buddhist practitioner who has vowed to help all beings reach enlightenment before he or she reaches enlightenment. Here Thrangu Rinpoche gives a very clear and lucid account of that hard-to-define topic of "emptiness" and "non-self." Finally, he gives a clear and lucid description of what is perhaps the most misunderstood level of

Buddhist practice—the vajrayāna. Being an accomplished vajrayāna practitioner, he is able to describe this level in practical terms.

Throughout this book Thrangu Rinpoche points out that all three of the vehicles of practice were practiced and preserved in Tibet. He also makes the important observation that no level is superior or "higher" than any other level. These levels are just three different ways that the Buddha gave for individuals to practice the Buddhist dharma. Which level one takes depends entirely on one's own needs, inclinations, and capabilities.

Clark Johnson, Ph. D.

The First Vehicle of Buddhist Practice

The Hīnayāna Path

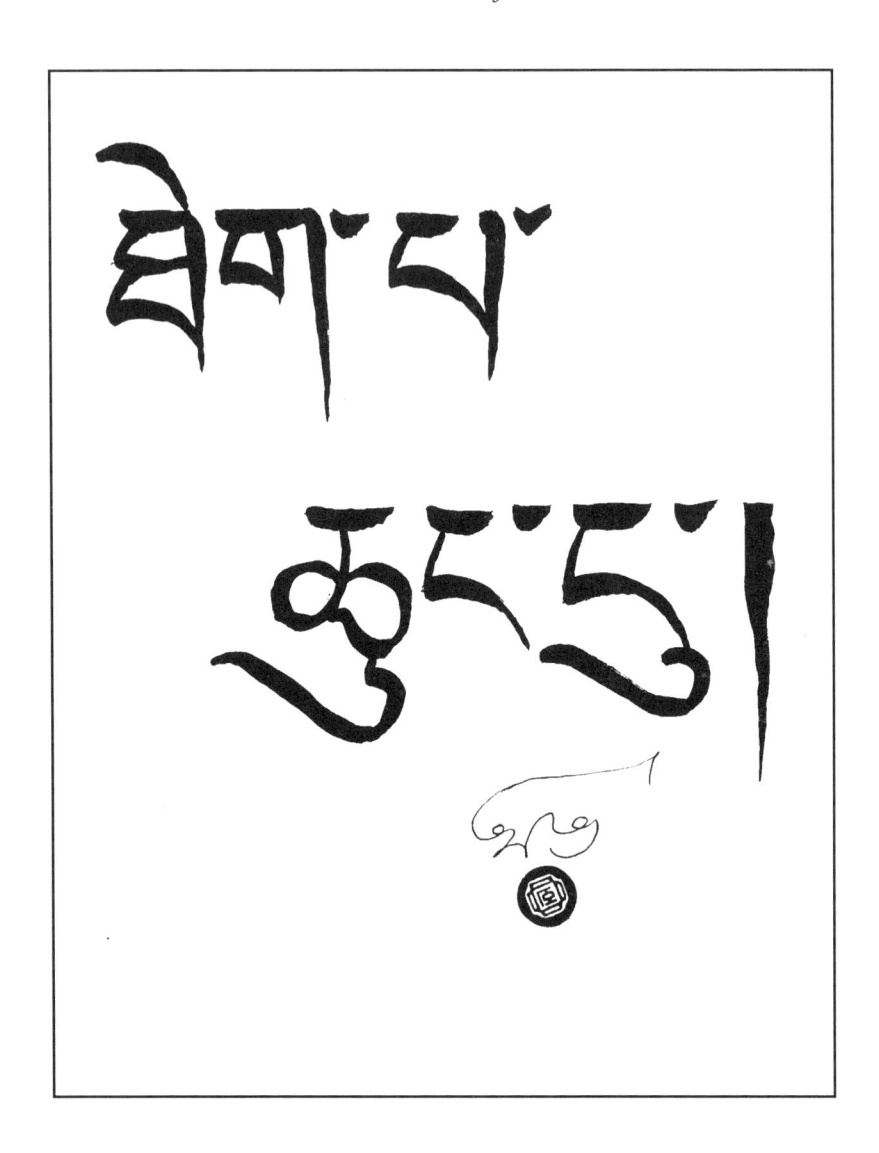

Thegpa chung ngu
by
Thrangu Rinpoche

Chapter 1

The Hīnayāna Path

Some say Tibetan Buddhism is the practice of *mahāyāna*[1] Buddhism. Others say that Tibetan Buddhism is actually the practice of *vajrayāna* Buddhism. Really one cannot say that Tibetan Buddhism is just mahāyāna or just vajrayāna Buddhism. The teachings of *dharma* in Tibet are called the "three immutables" or the "three-fold vajra" meaning the dharma of Tibet contains the teachings of the *hīnayāna*, of the mahāyāna as well as of the vajrayāna. More specifically, Tibetan Buddhism has the outer practice of the hīnayāna, the inner motivation or *bodhicitta* of the mahāyāna and the view and practice of the vajrayāna known as the secret or essential view. This is why it is necessary to study these three main levels or vehicles (Skt. *yānas*) of Buddhist practice.

One needs to understand that when the Buddha taught, he was not teaching as a great scholar who wanted to demonstrate a particular philosophical point of view or to teach for its own sake. His desire was to present the very essence of the deep and vast teachings of realization.For this reason he gave teachings which matched the abilities of his disciples. All the teachings he gave, some long and some short, were a direct and appropriate response to the development of the disciples who came to listen to him. Of course, people have very different capacities and different levels of understanding. They also have very different wishes and desires to learn and understand the dharma. If the Buddha had taught only the very essence of his own understanding of those vast and far-reaching teachings, then apart from a small number of disciples who had great intelligence and diligence, few people would have ever entered the path. The Buddha taught whatever allowed a person to develop spiritually and progress gradually towards liberation. When we analyze all the Buddha's teachings, we see that they fall into three main approaches or vehicles.

The Buddha's teachings helped each student in a way appropriate for the level he or she was at. Because of that, one finds that on the *relative level*[2] each student received some benefit from what Buddha taught. On the *absolute level,* one finds all of the Buddha's teachings have the same goal. When one analyzes the Buddha's teachings on the relative level, one finds that there are three levels. But, when one examines them from the absolute level, one sees there is only one level because all beings are directed towards the same goal.

The Hīnayāna

Of the three yānas the first is the hīnayāna. Hīnayāna literally means "lesser vehicle" but this term should in no way be a reproach or be construed to in any way diminish the importance of these teachings. In fact, the teachings of the hīnayāna are very important because they suit the capacities and development of a great number of students. If it weren't for these teachings, which are particularly appropriate for those who have limited wisdom or diligence, many persons would never been able to travel the mahāyāna path. Without the hīnayāna teachings there would be no way for practitioners to enter the dharma because they would not have had a way to enter the Buddhist path. This path is similar to a staircase: the lower step is the first step. This doesn't mean it is not important or should be ignored because without these lower steps one can never gain access to the upper stories. It should be very clear that this term "lesser" vehicle is in no way a pejorative term. It provides the necessary foundation on which to build.

The fundamental teachings of the hīnayāna are the main subject matter of the first *dharmacakra* or turning of the *wheel of dharma*. These teachings were given mainly in India in the town of Varanasi which is now called Benares. The main subject matter of these teachings is the *four noble truths*.

The Four Noble Truths

For the Buddha to have taught his disciples principally by demonstrating his miraculous abilities and powers would not have been the best way to establish them on the path of liberation. The best way to bring them to that wisdom and liberation was to point out the very truth of things; to point out the way things really are. So he taught the four noble truths and the two truths (relative and absolute truth). By seeing the way things really are, the students learned how to eliminate their mistakes and their delusions. Eliminating one's mistakes and delusions automatically destroys the causes of one's suffering and hardships. This allows one to reach progressively the state of liberation and great wisdom. That is why the four noble truths and the two truths are the essence of the first teachings of the Buddha.

The First Noble Truth

The first noble truth is the full understanding of suffering. Of course, in an obvious way, people are aware of suffering and know when they have unpleasant sensations such as hunger, cold, or sickness. But the first noble truth includes awareness of all the ramifications of suffering because it encompasses the very nature of suffering. This includes knowledge of the subtle and the obvious aspects of suffering. The obvious aspect of suffering is immediate pain or difficulty in the moment. Subtle suffering is more difficult to recognize because it begins with happiness. But by its very nature this happiness must change because it can't go on forever. Because it must change into suffering, this subtle suffering is the impermanence of pleasure. For example, when I went to Bhutan with His Holiness Karmapa, I was invited to the palace of the king of Bhutan. The palace of the king was magnificent, the king's chambers were beautiful, there were many servants who showed complete respect and obedience. But we found that even though there was so much external beauty, the king himself was suffering a great deal mentally. The king said that he was quite relieved that His Holiness had come and emphasized how much the visit meant to him because of the various difficulties with which he had been troubled. This is the subtle aspect of suffering. One thinks that a particular situation will give one the most happiness one can ever imagine, but actually, within the situation, there is a tremendous amount of anguish. If one thinks of those who are really fortunate—gods or human beings with a very rich and healthy life—it seems as though they have nothing but happiness. It is hard to understand that the very root, the very fiber of what is taking place is suffering because the situation is subject to change.

What is happiness? By its very nature it can often mean that there will be suffering later on. There is no worldly happiness that lasts for a very long time. Worldly happiness includes an element of change, of built-in suffering. For that reason the first noble truth of the awareness of suffering refers not just to immediate suffering, but also to the subtle elements of suffering. The Buddha taught the truth of suffering because everything that takes place on a worldly level is a form of suffering.

If one is suffering but is not aware of it, one will never have the motivation to eliminate this suffering and will continue to suffer. When one is aware of suffering, one can overcome it. With the more subtle forms of suffering, if one is happy and becomes aware that the happiness automatically includes the seed of suffering, then one will be much less inclined to become attached to this happiness. One will then think, "Oh, this seems to be happiness, but it has built-in suffering." Then one will want to dissociate from it. The first truth is that one should be aware of the nature of suffering. Once one has a very clear picture of the nature of suffering, one can really begin to avoid such suffering. Of course, everyone wants to avoid suffering and to emerge from suffering, but to accomplish this one needs to be absolutely clear about its nature.

When one becomes aware that the nature of day-to-day existence is suffering, one doesn't have to be miserable with the thought that suffering is always present. Suffering doesn't go on forever because the Buddha came into our world, gave teachings, and demonstrated clearly what suffering is. He also taught the means by which suffering can end and described a state of liberation which is beyond suffering. One does not have to endure suffering and can, in fact, be happy. Even though one cannot emerge immediately from suffering by practicing the Buddha's teachings, one can gradually eliminate suffering in this way, and move towards eventual liberation. This fact in itself can establish peace even before one has actually emerged completely from suffering. Applying the Buddha's teachings, one can be happy in the relative phase of one's progress and then at the end one will gain wisdom and liberation and be happy in the ultimate sense, as well.

The first noble truth makes it clear that there is suffering. Once we know what suffering is, we must eliminate that suffering. It is not a question of eliminating the suffering itself, but of eliminating the causes of suffering. Once we remove the causes of suffering, then automatically the effect, which is suffering, is no longer present. This is why to eliminate this suffering, we must become aware of the second noble truth, the truth of universal origination.

The Second Noble Truth

The truth of universal origination is an English translation of the name the Buddha gave to this noble truth. It means "that which is the cause or origin of absolutely everything." The truth of universal origination indicates that the root cause of suffering is *karma* and the *kleśas*. Karma is a Sanskrit word which means "activity" and kleśa in Sanskrit means "mental defilement" or "mental poison." If we do not understand the Buddha's teachings, we would most likely attribute all happiness and suffering to some external cause. We might think that happiness and suffering come from the environment, or from the gods, and that everything that happens originates in some source outside of one's control. If we believe this, it is extremely hard, if not impossible, to eliminate suffering and its causes. On the other hand, when we realize that the experience of suffering is a product of what we have done, that is, a result of one's actions, eliminating suffering becomes possible. Once we are aware of how suffering takes place, then we can begin to remove the causes of suffering. First we must realize that what we experience is not dependent on external forces, but on what we have done previously. This is the understanding of karma. Karma produces suffering and is driven by the defilements. The term "defilement" refers mainly to our negative motivation and negative thoughts which produce negative actions.

The Third Noble Truth

The third noble truth is the cessation of suffering through which the causes of karma and the defilements can be removed. We have control over suffering because karma and the defilements take place within us—we create them, we experience them. For that reason, we don't need to depend on anyone else to remove the cause of suffering. The truth of universal origination is that if we do unvirtuous actions, we are creating suffering. It also means that if we abandon unvirtuous actions, we remove the possibility of experiencing suffering in the future. What we experience is entirely in our hands. Therefore the Buddha has said that we should give up the causes of karma and the defilements. Virtuous actions result in happiness and unvirtuous actions result in suffering. This idea is not particularly easy to grasp because one can't see the whole process take place from beginning to end.

There are three kinds of actions: mental, verbal, and physical. These are subdivided into virtuous and unvirtuous physical actions, virtuous and unvirtuous verbal actions, and virtuous and unvirtuous mental actions. If one abandons these three types of unvirtuous actions, then one's actions become automatically virtuous.

There are three unvirtuous physical actions: the harming of life, sexual misconduct, and stealing. The results of these three unvirtuous actions can be observed immediately. For example, when there is a virtuous relationship between a man and woman who care about each other, who help each other, and have a great deal of love and affection for each other, they will be happy because they look after each other. Their wealth will usually increase and if they have children, their love and care will result in mutual love in the family. In the ordinary sense, happiness develops out of this deep commitment and bond they have promised to keep. Whereas, when there is an absence of commitment, there is also little care and sexual misconduct arises. This is not the ground out of which love arises, or upon which a home in which children can develop happiness can be built. One can readily see that a lack of sexual fidelity can create many kinds of difficulties.

One can also see the immediate consequences of other unvirtuous physical actions. One can see that those who steal have difficulties and suffer; those who don't steal experience happiness and have a good state of mind. Likewise, those who kill create many problems and unhappiness for themselves, while those who support life are happy.

The same applies to one's speech although it is not so obvious. But on closer examination, one can also see how happiness develops out of virtuous speech and unhappiness results from unvirtuous speech. At first, lying may seem to be useful because one might think that one can deceive others and gain some advantage. But the Sakya Paṇḍita said that this is not true. If one lies to one's enemies or persons one doesn't get along with very well, because they are one's enemies they are not going to take notice of what one is saying anyway. It will be quite hard to deceive them. If they are one's friends, one might be able to deceive them at first by telling a lie. But after the first time, they won't trust you any more and may think that you have been a hypocrite. Lying doesn't really work. Then if one looks at the opposite, a person who takes pains to speak the truth will develop a reputation of being a truthful person and out of this trust many good things will emerge.

Once we have considered the example of the consequences of lying, we can think of similar consequences relating to other kinds of damaging speech: slander, and coarse, aggressive, and useless speech. Except for the immediate and the short-termed consequences, virtuous speech produces happiness and unvirtuous speech produces suffering. When we say "useless speech," we mean speech that is really useless, not just conversational. So, if we have a good mind and want someone to relax and be happy, even though the words may not be of great meaning, our words are based on the idea of benefit and goodness. By useless speech we mean chatter for no reason at all. Worse than that is "chatter rooted in the defilements" when we say bad things about other people because of a dislike or jealousy of them. One just gossips about the character of people. That is really useless speech. Besides being useless, this very often causes trouble because it sets people against each other and causes bad feelings.

The same applies to "harmful speech." If there is really a loving and beneficial reason for talking, for example, scolding a child when the child is doing something dangerous or scolding a child for not studying in school, that is not harmful speech because it is devoid of the defilements, rather it is a skillful way of helping someone. If there is that really genuine, beneficial attitude and love behind what one says, it is not harmful speech. But if speech is related to the defilements such as aggression or jealousy, then it is harmful speech and is something to give up.

We can go on to examine the various states of mind and see that a virtuous mind produces happiness and unvirtuous states of mind create unhappiness. For instance, strong aggression will cause us to lose our friends. Because of our aggressiveness, our enemies will become even worse enemies and the situation will become inflamed. If we are aggressive and hurt others and they have friends, eventually those friends will also become enemies. On the other hand, goodness will arise through our caring for our loved ones and then extending this by wishing to help others. Through this they will become close and helpful friends. Through the power of our love and care, our enemies and people we don't get along with will improve their behavior and maybe those enemies will eventually become friends. If we have companions and wish to benefit others, we can end up with very good friends and all the benefits which that brings. In this way we can see how cause and effect operate, how a virtuous mind brings about happiness and how an unvirtuous mind brings about suffering and problems.

There are two main aspects of karma: one related to experience and one related to conditioning. The karma relating to experience has already been discussed. Through unvirtuous physical actions we will experience problems and unhappiness. Likewise, through unvirtuous speech such as lying, we will experience unhappiness and sorrow. Through a unvirtuous state of mind, we will also experience unhappiness as was demonstrated by the example of an aggressive attitude. All of this is related to the understanding that any unvirtuous activity produces unhappiness and pain.

The second aspect of karma relates to conditioning. By acting unvirtuously with our body, speech, or mind, we habituate ourself to a certain style of behavior. Unvirtuous physical or verbal behaviors add to the habit of doing things. For example, each time one kills, one is conditioned to kill again. If one lies, that increases the habit of lying. An aggressive mind conditions one's mind so one becomes more aggressive. In later lives, that conditioning will be reborn with a great tendency to kill, to lie, to engage in sexual misconduct, and so on. These are the two aspects to karma. One is the direct consequence of an act and the other is the conditioning that creates a tendency to engage in behavior of that kind. Through these two aspects karma produces all happiness and suffering in life.

Even though we may recognize that unvirtuous karma gives rise to suffering and virtuous karma gives rise to happiness, it is hard for us to give up unvirtuous actions and practice virtuous actions because the defilements exercise a powerful influence on us. We realize that suffering is caused by unvirtuous karma, but we can't give up the karma itself. We need to give up the defilements because they are the root of unvirtuous actions. To give up the defilements means to give up unvirtuous actions of body (such as killing, stealing, and sexual misconduct), the unvirtuous actions of speech (such as lying, slander and harmful and useless speech), and the unvirtuous aspects of mind (such as aggression, attachment, or ignorance). Just wanting to give up the defilements does not remove them. However, the Buddha in his great kindness and wisdom has given us a very skillful way to eliminate the very root of all the defilements through the examination of the belief in the existence of an ego or a self.

A Belief in a Self

We cannot easily understand this belief in a self because it is very deep-rooted. But if we search for this self that we believe in, we will discover that the self does not actually exist. Then with careful examination we will be able to see through this false belief in a self. When this is done, the defilements are diminished and with the elimination of a belief in self, negative karma is also eliminated.

This belief in a self is a mistaken perception. It's an illusion. For example, if one has a flower and were to interrogate one hundred people about it, they would all come to the same conclusion that it is indeed a flower. So one could be pretty sure that it is a flower. But, if one asked a person "Is this me?" he would say, "No, it's you." A second person would say, "It's you." One would end up with one hundred persons who say its "you" and only oneself would consider it as "me." So statistically one's self is not verifiable through objective means.

We also tend to think of "me" as one thing, as a unity. When we examine what we think of as ourselves, we find it is made up of many different components: the various parts of the body, the different organs, and the different elements. There are so many of them, yet we have this feeling of a single thing which is "me." When we examine any of these components and try to find something that is the essence of self, the self cannot be found in any of these parts. By contemplating this and working through it very thoroughly, we begin to see how this "I" is really a composite.

Once we have eliminated this incorrect way of thinking, the idea of an "I" becomes easy to get rid of. So, all of the desire rooted in thinking, "I must be made happy" can be eliminated as well as all the aversion rooted in the idea of "this difficulty must be eliminated." Through the elimination of the idea of "I" we can annihilate the defilements. Once the defilements are gone, then the negative karma which is rooted in the defilements will cease. Once the negative karma ceases, suffering will no longer take place. This is why Buddha said that the root of suffering needs to be abandoned.

The first two noble truths may be summed up with two statements:

One should be aware of and know what suffering is.
One should give up the origin of suffering.

To summarize, once one recognizes what suffering really is, then one begins by removing its causes. One stops doing unvirtuous actions which create suffering. To stop these unvirtuous activities, one eliminates them at their root which is the defilements and various unhealthy attitudes. To eradicate the defilements one needs to remove their heart, which is the belief in a self. If one does that, then one will eventually come to realize the wisdom of non-self. By understanding the absence of a self, one no longer creates the defilements and bad actions and brings an end to that whole process. This is highly possible to reach; therefore there is the third noble truth, the truth of cessation.

The very essence and nature of cessation is peace (Tib. *she wa*).[3] Sometimes people think of Buddhahood in terms of brilliant insights or something very fantastic. In fact, the peace one obtains from the cessation of everything unhealthy is the deepest happiness, bliss, and well-being. Its very nature is lasting in contrast to worldly happiness which is exciting for a time, but then changes. In contrast, this ultimate liberation and omniscience is a very deeply moving peace. Within that peace all the powers of liberation and wisdom are developed. It is a very definitive release from both suffering and its effect and is a definitive release from the defilements which are the cause of suffering. There are four main qualities of this truth of cessation. First, it is the cessation of suffering. Second, it is peace. Third, it is the deepest liberation and wisdom. Fourth, it is a very definitive release from saṃsāra. Cessation is a product of practicing the path shown to us by the Most Perfect One, the Buddha. The actual nature of that path is the topic of the fourth noble truth, which is called the truth of the path because it describes the path that leads to liberation.

The Fourth Noble Truth

The fourth noble truth is called "the truth of the path" because the path leads us to the ultimate goal. We do this step by step, stage by stage, progressively completing our journey. The main stages of Buddhism are called the "*five paths*" because by progressively traversing them we eventually reach our destination which is cessation. This path of the Buddha can be analyzed through its five main stages which are called the five paths (Skt. *marga)*. The names of the five paths are the stage of accumulation, the stage of junction, the stage of insight, the stage of cultivation, and the stage of nonstudy. Properly speaking, the first four of these are the path with the fifth one being the fruition of the other four paths.

The Five Paths

The first path is called the "path of accumulation" because we gather or accumulate a great wealth of many things. This is the stage in which we try to gather all the positive factors which enable us to progress. We try to cultivate diligence, the good qualities, and the wisdom which penetrates more deeply into the meaning of things. We commit ourselves to accumulate all the various positive aspects of practice. We gather the positive elements into our being while at the same time working in many different ways to remove all the unwanted elements from one's life. We also apply various techniques to eliminate the various blockages and obstacles which are holding us back. This is called the stage of accumulation because we engage in this manifold activity which gathers these new things into our life.

In ordinary life we are caught up in the level of worldliness. Even though we don't want to be, we are still operating on a level of conditioned existence (Skt. *saṃsāra*) because we are still under the influence of the defilements. They have a very strong habitual grip on our existence. We need to get rid of these defilements in order to find our way out of saṃsāra. Of course, we want to find happiness and peace and we know it is possible. But even with the strongest will in the world, we cannot do it overnight. It is like trying to dye a large cloth in that one needs to bring many different elements together to change its color.

So, first of all, in order to gain the good qualities, we need to work on creating all the different conditions which will make these qualities emerge. To develop the various insights of meditation and real wisdom, we need to develop great faith and confidence in the validity and usefulness of this wisdom. Once we are convinced of its value, we need to change our habits so that we have the diligence to do all the things necessary to make insight and wisdom emerge. Therefore, there are many factors and conditions we must generate within our life to bring about our happiness.

To remove all the unwholesome factors binding us in saṃsāra, we must uproot belief in a solid self, eliminate the various defilements which hinder us, and bring together the many different conditions that make this transformation and purification possible. We talk about accumulation because we are assembling all the different conditions that make this transformation possible. We won't be able to progress in a significant manner until we have gathered all these causes and conditions properly, completely and perfectly within ourselves. For that reason the purpose of this stage of accumulation is to complete all the necessary conditions by gathering them into our existence.

Eventually, because of the complete gathering of favorable conditions, we will reach the third path which is the "path of insight." This is the stage during which insight into the true nature of phenomena are developed. This insight is beyond the veil of delusion. Linking the path of accumulation and the path of insight is the second path of junction. Here our inner realization, the very way we perceive things, begins to link up with the truth of the actual nature of phenomena because we are gathering all the favorable circumstances that will eventually lead us to the actual insight itself. When we attain insight into the way things really are and this insight develops beyond the level of delusion and mistaken views, we realize that there is no self. Once there is no longer a belief in self, there are no longer any root defilements of attachment, aggression, or ignorance associated with the false belief in a solid self. Once there are no longer any defilements, we do nothing unvirtuous and have no more suffering.

Now, it is true that once we have that insight, all suffering is immediately removed, but in another way, that is not true. This is because the delusion of a self is a habit which has been built up for such a long time and is very, very hard to remove. For example, when we have realized that an unchanging self is a delusion fabricated by our mind, still when we hit our finger with a hammer, we experience pain. We still have the feeling, "I am suffering" because there is an enduring built-up association of "I" with the flesh of our body. Removal of that long established conditioning of self occurs through a long process of cultivating the truth of non-self. This is the fourth stage of the cultivation of insight.

The fourth stage is called the path of cultivation (*gom lam* in Tibetan). The word *gom* is usually translated as "meditation" but actually means "to get used to something" or "to accustom oneself."[4] This is why it is translated here as "the path of cultivation," while other texts translate it as "the path of meditation." But in this stage its the insight into the nature of things and getting used to that insight. By becoming more and more familiar with the truth of phenomena, we can remove the very fine traces of defilements and the subconscious conditioning that still exist. Through gradual working on these, the goal of enlightenment will be attained.

Through the cultivation of insight we eventually reach the goal of the fifth path which is called "the path of no more study." Through cultivation we remove even the most subtle causes of suffering. Once this is completed we have reached the highest state and there are no more new paths to traverse making this "the path of no more study" or "the path of no more practice."

To the first two quotations from the Buddha which have already been presented, two more can be added to sum up the last two noble truths:

One should be aware of and know what suffering is.
One should give up the origin of suffering.
One should make cessation of suffering manifest.
One should establish the path thoroughly in one's being.

We need to make the truth of cessation real, to manifest it in ourselves. We can't just make it manifest by wishing, hoping, or praying for it. We can't just pray to the *three jewels* (the Buddha, dharma and *saṅgha*) for cessation and through their kindness they will just give it to us. The law of cause and effect, karma, makes that impossible. To attain the goal of cessation, we must be thoroughly established on the path and the path must be properly and thoroughly developed in ourselves.

One may wonder if the five paths overlap. Generally speaking, for nearly everyone, the stages of the path are consecutive and separate. Having finished the first stage, one progresses to the second stage and so on. Some texts in the *Abhidharma* and the *Kindrug* say that there are some individuals who can travel the paths simultaneously. But they are very exceptional persons; most persons need to complete one path at a time. For instance, in the path of accumulation one can start on the work that is primarily associated with the path of junction, developing insight into the truth. The principle purpose for separating these two stages is to enumerate the positive factors one must gather to complete the path of accumulation and to distinguish them from the development of insight and the level of the path of junction. These paths are not completely separate. So one cannot say they do not overlap, that there aren't several things taking place at the same time.

These four truths taught by the Buddha are very important. One can compare them to someone who is sick. When someone is sick and has much discomfort, the first thing to do is to investigate the nature of the problem. What is the sickness? Is it in the brain? In the heart? etc. One needs to locate the actual problem and investigate the symptoms of the illness. Then in order to cure that person one also needs to know what is producing the disease. Only by attacking the cause of the symptoms can one actually cure the person. This is a very good analogy for the first two noble truths. One needs to understand the nature of suffering and to know just what it entails. But just understanding the problem is not enough to bring an end to the suffering because one also needs to understand the causes of suffering, which are karma and the defilements. Then one needs to be able to eradicate the causes.

The inspiration to overcome illness is, of course, to understand all the qualities of good health and to be free from the sickness. To continue the example, the Buddha shows one all the qualities of cessation (enlightenment); that is a healthy and wonderful thing. Once one knows that the remedy exists, then one applies the remedy to what has been blocking the state of good health. One applies the very skillful remedies of the path making it possible to deal with karma and the defilements in order to obtain that good mental health. For that reason the last two truths are like the medicine whose result is cessation of suffering.

The order of working through the four noble truths is not a chronological order. They are ordered logically to help us understand. The first two truths relate to suffering and its cause (saṃsāra). First of all, the character of suffering is explained. Once one understands the character of suffering, one will want to know what causes it so the suffering can be eliminated. The second two truths are related to *nirvāṇa*. These are not arranged in order of experience because the cause of suffering must obviously come before the suffering itself.

Meditation in the Hīnayāna

When one studies the hīnayāna, one studies it in the beginning from the viewpoint of intellectual understanding. Then through meditation practice, one investigates the results that emerge. The four noble truths, which are the heart of the hīnayāna are the view of the hīnayāna. The principle focus of hīnayāna practice is the validity of the four noble truths. The actual practice of meditation within the hīnayāna is a little bit different from the understanding of the truths themselves. When one understands suffering and its causes, one realizes that as long as one is involved with worldly affairs, one will continue creating the causes of suffering, which means one will be reborn over and over again in this vortex of saṃsāra. Therefore the way out is to cut this attachment to saṃsāra. There are several meditation practices which enable one to do this.

Meditational Practices

The principle practice which enables one to cut attachment to saṃsāra is to meditate on the impermanent nature of saṃsāra. By meditating on impermanence, one will be less inclined to become involved in worldly activities. Attachment becomes less attractive as one begins to appreciate how quickly circumstances change. One can see that even though kings and heroes of the past might have been very famous and wealthy, their fame and wealth did not go on forever but eventually ended. In meditation one contemplates people and the changes they endure; one contemplates objects and their changes and the ways in which they change. When one sees that there is nothing that stays the same, one realizes activities and objects in saṃsāra are not worth that much involvement and attachment. The liberation of the mind then begins to take place. One does not completely give up everything overnight but realizes that too much involvement and attachment are not very beneficial. One realizes that it's not worth spending much time with samsaric conditioning.

The second principle meditation practice is on the nature of suffering in saṃsāra. Previously, it has been explained how one can experience directly the actual emergence of suffering. As explained before, things which seem quite pleasant initially, by their very nature, must bring about suffering later. One realizes that suffering is inherent even in pleasant things. Therefore this contemplation on suffering, which is part of all samsaric phenomena, is the second point. It helps one realize not to spend so much time and involvement in worldly things. It also helps one to realize that by devoting energy to these contemplations one can profit greatly.

The third main meditation is on emptiness and the fourth meditation is on the absence of ego or self. As was explained previously, meditation on emptiness is mainly concerned with realizing that the inner phenomena which one thinks of as "mine" and the outer phenomena which one thinks of as "belonging to me" has no validity. The fourth meditation on non-self is concerned more with the idea of the "self" itself, the owner of those things, and how this idea of self is a delusion.

The Examination of the Self

One must separate the idea of self from the cause from which it springs. The idea of the self is principally derived from a deluded apprehension of the *skandhas* or aggregates that amass from different things. The various skandhas, of which we are composed, are made up of many, many different individual elements. Because of the gross way in which we perceive, we can't see all the minute and brief elements which make up existence. We tend to lump them together and see them as just one thing. Once we see many things as one, we tend to name it, define it, and give it an identity. So when we see things with our perception we do not see many minute, short-lived components, but tend to see them as a whole and solidify them as real and existent. It is because we relate to gross wholes and give them an identity that we develop this idea of a self.

Beginningless Time

We also have a problem with time. There is no point at which we could say, "At this point there wasn't that delusion and then at this point this mistaken view took place." The mistake is beginningless. When we first see this word "beginningless" in Buddhist texts, it seems a rather unusual idea that a delusion could not have a beginning. However, if we examine almost anything we find it is beginningless. For example, take a brass pot.[5] It was probably made in India, but that was not its beginning because in India it was made from brass. That brass came from ore and we can trace the ore back through time by tracing all the minute particles of which it is made up going back forever. Nearly everything we examine is beginningless. So it is the same with the concept of self. If we trace it back, we keep going back and back and back. It is not as though there is one point in which we were clear and in the next moment delusion suddenly occurred. We can just never find the beginning. It is something happening all the time because of the grossness of our perception and the mistaken consciousness that labels the objects of perception.

For instance, consider the example of a flower and its seed. This example demonstrates that one thing originates from another. Now there is a flower but when we trace back, we find there was a seed and the seed itself came from a flower and so on. The same with a brass pot, we can trace it back to some geological time and never find a point where the pot actually began. The point is that it is beginningless. When we examine our own existence, we say there is suffering because of karma and that there is karma because of the defilements and the defilements are there because of ignorance. But we cannot find one point where this process began because if we trace it back we find that each step involves more history. We can keep going back and back and each event has even more history behind it and so on. That is why we say it is "beginningless" because we cannot answer the question, "What happened in the beginning?" It is not as though there was one ignorant thought and that was the beginning of everything. Ignorance is taking place continually and has been occurring since this beginning without beginning. Ignorance is then a continuing mistaken perception of the minute aggregates. We conceptualize the idea of a thing which isn't there except in the mind of the observer. That is the actual process of ignorance which takes place over and over again. Even though there are so many different components in the skandhas, we conceive them as a mistaken "I." Perceiving the millions and millions of particles of the pot as a single idea of "a pot" is a mistaken perception. This faulty perception continues into the future and we can trace it back into the past. The inability to perceive correctly is continuous, that process occurs again and again. All the problems have come from that ignorance. We can never find a beginning but it does have an end because once we pierce this delusion and reach the truth, we can find liberation from this deluded process.

The Skandhas

We can make that split between the percept and what is perceived. At the beginning we may think that the perceiver is the actual self and the delusion involves only the object of perception. But actually when we examine the perception of the perceiver, we discover that this same mistake is taking place. The many minute particles are mistaken for solid things. An analysis of the five skandhas reveals that the first skandha deals with form and the way in which things are perceived externally. The other four skandhas deal with the internal mind—feelings, the process of perception, cognition, and consciousness. There are many elements that come together which can be mistaken for a self in just the same way one mistakes collections of minute particles as just one thing. For instance, if we look at the skandha of consciousness, there are many different elements of consciousness and they are always changing. For example, we have happy feelings, unpleasant feelings, fearful feelings and so on. When we look at all the contradictions which make up the mind, we see that there is not just one unique, unchanging perceiver, but that the perceiving mind is made up of many different changing elements. We could never say any one of these are consciousness of a self. If there were a self, we could say, "Oh, yes, that is definitely the self, that is the consciousness of a self." In fact, what we sometimes think of as the "I" is a feeling associated with happiness or sadness or a certain kind of consciousness.

Sometimes the "I" seems to be the body, sometimes the "I" seems to be the mind which perceives the body, sometimes it seems to be both. That is why the perception of a self is a delusion. The "I" is never constant. It is simply an idea associated with what is happening. If it were the same all the time, then we could point to it very clearly and say, "This is I." But when we think about "I" or when we talk about "I" we continually shift from one identification to another never really establishing what is "I." Once there is this delusion of "I," there is the idea of "mine" and the process becomes even more complicated.

The Self in Reincarnation

We may wonder if there is no "self," then what is it that passes on in reincarnation.[6] There is reincarnation, but this reincarnation is not particularly linked to a self or ego. It is not that there is a self which creates one life after another so that one develops the idea, "I have been reborn, I have been somebody else before I was reborn." But actually what transmigrates is not the same self; it is not the same "I" which crops up again and again or the same "I" which provokes all these different rebirths.

To explain what actually happens, the Buddha taught the idea of interdependence or what is also called "*interdependent origination.*" Interdependent origination explains the arising of one thing from another; how one thing depends upon another for its existence. For example, a flower comes from a seed. There is a seed which makes a shoot. The shoot sprouts leaves which eventually become flowers. The flower will then create more seeds and so on. So there is a continuity, but apart from this continuity there are great differences between the seed and the flower in shape, color, nature, etc. So there is a continuity which is a process of dependence and a process of origination. Change takes place all the time within the context of this dependence. In the same way ignorance occurs, and because of ignorance certain actions and activities follow. And because of these actions eventually there will be some sort of rebirth. Because of the rebirth there is aging, sickness, death, and so on. All of these factors are interdependent. One is caused by the other. There is a continuum, but there is not one thing which carries on and one thing that is unchanging. The Buddha taught that what happens from one lifetime to another occurs because of interdependence, not a "self" which is an entity that goes on and on manifesting continuously.

To understand this form of transmigration, the fact that there have been so many different Karmapas[7] does not mean that they are emanations of a self. First we must examine the deluded idea of self on the level of ordinary people. We think, "This is me, this is my one life and it has been one single life." We think we have a self which is this life. However, when we examine this life, we find everything is changing; we do not have the same physical body; when we were a tiny baby we were only two feet tall, later growing to five feet tall. The same is true of our mind. When we were a baby, we could not even say our mother's name and were very ignorant. When we grew up, we learned to read and write and our mind underwent a tremendous change. We take this "me" and "mine" as being ourself. However, when we look at this carefully, apart from the continuity that took place from one step to the other, there is not a single thing that stayed the same. Nevertheless, we tend to think of "me" as though "me" had been the same all the time. That is how we are incorrect about ordinary people and about ourselves. The same is true of *tulkus* and the great *rinpoches*. Apart from the fact that there is a continuity of their noble mind and their activity which benefits beings, there is no self, no constant entity which is continuously present. Because we are deluded, we think of them as being one fixed person.

The word *skandha* is a Sanskrit word for "aggregate" or "heap" and provides an image of a pile of different things. Because it is a whole heap, we can say, "This is one pile." But when we examine the heap carefully, we discover it includes many different types of things. Yet from the gross point of view we globalize and think of a heap as just one entity and relate to it as if it were just one thing. So when we examine our own existence and what is taking place from one lifetime to another, we can find individual instances of many different things, so many different minutiae. Because there are so many different elements, our gross perception tends to label them as simply "I." This process of contemplating the skandhas shows us how this delusion of self occurs. It is like a mountain which consists of many different pieces of dirt and dust. One gives this the name "mountain" even though it is made up of millions of different particles. Because we have developed the idea of "I," we also develop desire and these desires eventually lead to the defilements that cause suffering. The liberation from suffering (enlightenment) consists in the realization that this "I" is a delusion, a mistake, and that there is no "I" or a permanent self. Once we have seen through that, there is no more "I" to want anything, no more "I" to dislike anything, no more "I" to possess the defilements, and therefore no more negative karma.

We shouldn't take the continuity as being a thing. When we have the delusion of a self, for instance, between being a baby and a grown person, many things change and are different, yet we have this deluded projection about self which appears to be the same. We might say that the "I" has been there all the time but this is not true because the continuum is not the same as an idea of self. It is not that there is a continuum which carries on in something, which would be another word for self. A continuum by its very continuity implies change and difference. So a continuum is tracing the way one thing changes into another and then into something else. We follow through the connection of one thing to another. But it doesn't mean that because there is a continuity, there is something which is the same and present all the time. So with reincarnated lamas there is just this unbroken Buddha activity.

This also happens when one dies. When one dies, one's body is no longer useful but one's mind carries on. It is not as though there is a mind as a fixed thing that carries on and on. It is that there is a continuity; one can trace the change from one state of mind to another and that is what carries on. That mind carries on through future lives, but it is not as though there is a constant thing like a self or a continuum which is nothing more than a synonym for self.

To summarize, impermanence, suffering, emptiness, and absence of ego are the four main aspects of meditation which helps us to realize the truth of suffering. When we understand more about the emptiness of phenomena, we begin to see the absence of ego automatically and we will have less aggression, attachment, and ignorance. When these diminish, there will be less suffering.

Meditation on the Four Noble Truths

There is nothing wrong with worldly happiness and all the good and nice things in life *per se.* It is very good to be happy and content and to gain happiness from life. The only problem comes when we are trying to train ourselves for something higher, deeper, and more beneficial; if we become too involved with happiness and the good things of life, then they will hold us back from our training and development. It is like a young child. If the child is playing, the child and parents are very happy. There is nothing at all wrong with that. But if the child is going to grow up, obviously the child has to learn his lessons and go to school. If the lessons are jeopardized because the child is playing all the time, he or she will never develop and go onto something useful and productive.

Likewise, worldly things are not bad in themselves, but if we are aiming for something deeper and beneficial, we do not take too much time being involved with worldly things.

The realization of the truth is very slow because we are apathetic. The remedy to this apathy is to realize the four noble truths completely, not just a little. When we clearly see the first truth of suffering and realize what it is and how much there is to it, we will really work to remove the causes and actually traverse the path. It is the wisdom of seeing things as they are which causes us to develop our practice. When the Buddhist teachings say that we need to leave saṃsāra, they point to the urgency of getting out of saṃsāra. It is not that they are saying we have to give up eating, wearing clothes, and other worldly things. Rather we should not have great involvement and attachment to saṃsāra.

The understanding of the second noble truth of universal origination involves two meditations. These two are realizing the existence of interdependent origination and realizing the complete manifestation of interdependent origination. For the first meditation one realizes that karma and the defilements are the cause of all suffering and suffering doesn't come from outer conditions, but rather from one's previous karma. For the second meditation one realizes that karma comes from the defilements, so one realizes the universal origination of suffering. Then one sees how powerful karma is in one's life and this is the complete manifestation of origination.

For the truth of cessation, one meditates to appreciate what happens once all these difficulties and their causes have been removed. One meditates on the cessation from the view of taking away all these blocks and veils so the good qualities will emerge. One meditates on how one can eliminate suffering and the cause of suffering. Through this one realizes the positive quality of this cessation which is the very best peace for oneself. Realizing cessation is possible and these positive qualities will emerge and inspire one to strive on the path and develop all the qualities of peace.

There are four main points to meditation on the fourth noble truth which is the path. One needs first to contemplate the presence and validity of the path to develop an intelligent awareness of the path itself and to realize that without the path of dharma one will never achieve complete liberation or freedom from one's problems. Next one needs to be very aware of the value of the path in relation to other activities. Third, by realizing its value, one needs to actually put the path into practice. Finally, one needs to contemplate how the path is a complete release from saṃsāra. It is actually the path which leads one to freedom from all the problems of saṃsāra.

Practice of the Hīnayāna Path

The key word in the practice of the hīnayāna path is the *Vinaya*[8] which in Tibetan is *dul wa* which means "taming oneself." The word is very appropriate if we consider, for example, the taming of an elephant. An elephant is very wild at first and if we want to ride it, to get it to do work, or lead it somewhere, we can't do it. But by gradually taming the elephant we can ride it, we can get it to work, and we can lead it around. In fact, it becomes very docile and under our control. We can apply this analogy to ourself. At first our mind, body, and speech are very coarse and wild too. This means that just small physical irritations can cause us to flare up and fight. A little bit of verbal irritation upsets us and we begin to shout, scream, and abuse others. Small mental irritations make us think all sorts of nasty and aggressive things. So in the beginning, our mind is very wild and out of control. Hīnayāna practice is designed to train our mind so that eventually it becomes very docile and workable and we are able to cope properly with any situation.

The process of training is related to the commitments we make. We take certain vows and precepts to train ourselves. We do this because we have become used to doing unvirtuous actions and to get out of that habit, we make certain promises or commitments to do virtuous actions and bind ourselves to that virtuous activity. This is a very practical way of training ourselves to refrain from unvirtuous activities and accustoming ourselves gradually to virtuous activities. At first glance we may think that the commitments and vows are really restrictive and difficult and this keeps us from doing beneficial actions. It seems like being put into a straightjacket or a prison. Actually, it is not like that at all. The Sanskrit word for this training which covers making vows and commitments is *śīla* which means "coolness." That was translated into Tibetan as *tsultrim* which means "keeping one's discipline" in the way taught by the Buddha. This idea of coolness gives the impression of relaxation and easiness. This is a very good word because one can see that when one maintains virtue, this virtue creates happiness and leads to a pleasant and good situation. And when one practices unvirtuous activities of the body, it causes problems, difficulties, and hardships. Likewise, when one practices improper speech, more and more problems arise. By maintaining good and pure speech, very pleasant results emerge. The same applies to the mind. When one keeps the mind very pure, it brings much happiness. So when one thinks about it carefully, one can see that keeping the commitments, making promises, and restricting one's activities to virtuous ones is, in fact, the key to happiness. This is not at all a restriction or a difficult situation because it is the key to happiness. This is why the Sanskrit word *śīla* implies "calmness" or "pleasantness."

In order to understand the full power of the meaning of "coolness" for "discipline," one needs to think about its origins. The word comes from India which is a very hot country in the summer. When we say "coolness" in the West it does not strike us as a particularly good quality because it gets cold here. In Tibet they didn't translate it as "coolness" because Tibet is a very cold country. But in India coolness is a very valued quality. When the weather is very hot, it is very uncomfortable and one can't do what one wants. When one finds coolness in a hot place, one feels very happy and comfortable and one is in control. So when one is not committed to goodness, one has a lot of problems and is very uncomfortable and is not really in control of the situation. When one has this commitment to virtue, it is the key to happiness and one controls one's life. So that word "coolness" really gives a very vivid insight into the whole nature of self-control and good conduct.

The Buddha has given us certain commitments and vows to develop our good qualities and give up our bad qualities. But if we can't give up all the bad things totally, we shouldn't become depressed and think that there is no way we can practice the dharma. The Buddha in his compassion has given us many different kinds of commitments. We can take the vows of full ordination of a monk or nun[9] and commit ourself to a great deal of virtue and refrain from all unvirtuous things. If we can't manage that, there is the level of novice ordination. Then there are the eight layman's vows called the *genyan* vows in Tibetan. We don't have to take all eight vows, but can take one, two, or however many we can manage to practice. Even if we can't manage these vows for our whole life, we can make them for periods of time. We can observe the eight precepts for one day or a number of days such as while we are in retreat. So it is a very flexible situation that can be adopted by different persons according to their capacities.

The motivation of the hīnayāna practitioner is mainly concerned with working on his or her own happiness and liberation. At this level one is not especially concerned with helping everyone. Nevertheless, working principally for one's own emancipation is not a bad thing. In fact, it is a very good thing because if one is not able to help everyone, at least one is removing the suffering and its causes for oneself. There is nothing at all wrong with that. Of course, if one can work helping everyone, that is very wonderful. Actually, wishing to help others is not too workable until one has some degree of clarity and emancipation oneself. Therefore, working towards one's own purification is a very positive step on the journey towards eventually helping others. It is very good especially for individuals beginning the spiritual path, because it is much easier to think in terms of benefiting oneself. This is why the first wheel of dharma was the phase of the Buddha's teaching which was mainly concerned with showing the way to self-liberation.

The Second Vehicle of Buddhist Practice

The Mahāyāna Path

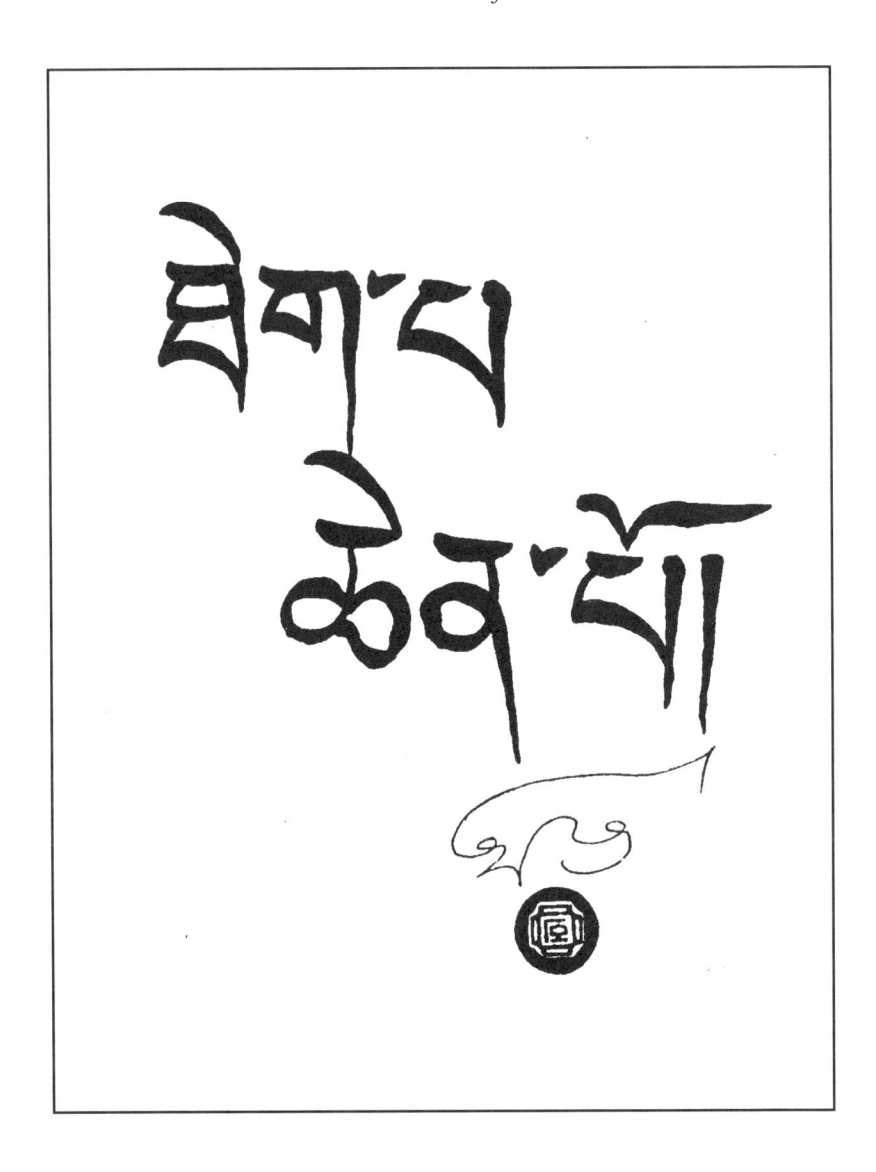

Tekpa chenpo
    by
        Thrangu Rinpoche

Chapter 2

The Mahāyāna

The Buddha taught the hīnayāna to beginning students because it was suitable for them. The second vehicle or yāna is the mahāyāna which means the "greater vehicle." It is called "great" because it involves very great motivation, a vast view, and an enormous practice.

The attitude of the *bodhisattva* who practices the mahāyāna is very great. First of all, he or she has an attitude of only wishing for good and virtuous things and not wishing anything which is unvirtuous or harmful to others. The hīnayāna practitioners have this good attitude, but it is a wish for their own progress and to have nothing bad happen to themselves. It is a healthy thing to wish good things and progress for oneself, but if one concentrates too much on that and tries to develop only self-interest there is the danger that it will eventually dominate other interests and one will use others for one's own ends and try to be better than them.

The attitude of the bodhisattva, the mahāyāna practitioner, is not being concerned just for oneself, but feeling the same concern for everyone. The reason a bodhisattva has unbiased love and compassion is that when we identify with a certain group and concentrate on its benefit, there is the danger we might harm others outside the group. Therefore, the mahāyāna path cultivates a completely unbiased love and compassion, caring equally for every being including nonhuman beings such as animals. Normally, we care for our friends and relatives and helping them may set others against us. Or we care for our race and set ourselves against other races or cultures. Or we care for humans and subjugate animals in order to make life better for mankind. All of this is the usual way of biased thought.

The mahāyāna approach is to care equally for any sentient being (which is any being who has a mind). This is because we realize that since beginningless time, each and every being has had the same basic wish to find happiness and to be free from suffering. In that respect, all beings are the same and therefore we try to help them equally.

The Four Immeasurables

The attitude of the bodhisattva is to want to help all beings find happiness and to relieve them of all their suffering. The bodhisattva doesn't believe there are some beings who want happiness and others who don't. The bodhisattva doesn't think that there are some who need to be freed from suffering and others who don't need to be freed from suffering. He or she realizes that absolutely all beings need to be helped to attain happiness and all beings need to be liberated from suffering. So the concern is for each and every being. In his commentaries, Patrul Rinpoche stressed the need for meditating on impartiality from the beginning of Buddhist practice. Normally, we meditate on the *four immeasurables* as they appear in the prayers which is in the order of limitless love, limitless compassion, limitless joy, and limitless impartiality. Patrul Rinpoche stresses the need for meditating on impartiality first because this removes the danger of having partial or biased love, partial or biased compassion. When we begin on the path, there is a strong tendency to have stronger love towards those we like and lesser love towards those we don't like. Once we have developed wisdom with this meditation, it becomes true love which cares for each and every person without any bias. This is the purest compassion because it cares for everyone.

We meditate first to cultivate impartiality, then we go on to meditate on great love, then on great compassion, and finally on *bodhicitta*. The first immeasurable, impartiality, means not being influenced by attachment or aggression. Great love means wanting everyone to attain happiness. Great compassion means wanting to free everyone from suffering. Bodhicitta, however, is more subtle as it is the wish to attain Buddhahood to help all beings. Its very nature is a loving and compassionate mind. What makes it subtle is that bodhicitta implies the development of wisdom (Skt. *prajña*). Without that wisdom, the love and compassion of the bodhisattva becomes incomplete love and incomplete compassion. With this incomplete love, one may really want to help others, but one may be ineffectual and may even harm the person one wants to help. With incomplete compassion one really wants to relieve the suffering of others and yet one doesn't know how to free them of their suffering. So, in the development of bodhicitta it is vital to develop one's wisdom and understanding along with one's love and compassion. This is the real meaning of bodhicitta which is the reason why it is subtle and hard to cultivate.

For example, suppose there were someone who was very hungry and we didn't have sufficient wisdom, we might think, "Oh, there's an easy solution, I can show him how to fish." We teach him how to fish and then in the short-term his hunger is alleviated and he can care for himself. However, we have shown him how to harm other beings[10] and so this act will create negative karma which will bring him nothing but trouble and difficulties in the future. So, even though our motivation was good and we exercised compassion, because of our ignorance, we weren't helping him at all, but made the situation worse. In other words, we need to act with love and compassion in a way that always brings good to all beings and takes into account the future implications of the act. This is the wisdom of the bodhisattva.

Another way of acting through love and compassion is not harming anyone. This is good in the short-term, but this doesn't result in lasting benefit. For example, we can give a poor person a gift of food and clothes. Although the motivation is good and it doesn't harm anyone, there is relatively little benefit because once the food or clothing are used up, the problem returns. What the bodhisattva aims for is a very great and lasting benefit. So when a bodhisattva helps someone, he or she tries always to give that person the very best, which is to establish them on the very best path. If we can show someone how to enter the supreme path, then the benefit is great and will increase not just immediately, but throughout all time. This doesn't harm others and helps the person develop in every aspect. So the love, compassion, and care that the bodhisattva has brings everyone to the supreme path and is really what is meant by true love, compassion, and the activity of the bodhisattva.

The bodhisattva's pure motivation is extremely powerful and skillful. For instance, communism also has a view or philosophy, but spreading that philosophy involved great armies, vast amounts of wealth, and a great deal of fighting and violence. Even all those armies and military equipment didn't really convince people of the truth of communism. In contrast, the Buddha didn't spend millions to propagate his ideas or employ vast armies with sophisticated weapons to convince people of the validity of what he was saying. He just had a begging bowl and taught. Because of his powerful and pure motivation, his ideas touched millions and millions of people and his teachings are still spreading. When the Buddha taught the dharma, he did it with the greatest love for everyone without any bias. He did it without wishing to bring harm to a single sentient being. He did it with a very pure compassion and wisdom. After 2,500 years all of his teachings are still perfectly intact and are still spreading and touching others without any effort on the Buddha's part showing the power of his pure motivation.

The bodhisattva's motivation of the mahāyāna is vast, far-reaching, and extremely powerful. Of all the things that one tries to awaken in the mahāyāna this motivation is really the key. From the very beginning one tries to develop this very vast and powerful attitude in which one develops love and compassion along with wisdom that is unbiased and a genuine desire to free everyone from suffering. This approach is the very core of bodhicitta, the driving force or motivation. The opposite of this is to have a biased mind and this selfish attitude poisons the environment. Bodhicitta, on the other hand, is very beneficial for oneself and for all others. So, when someone has bodhicitta, whatever he or she does, is like medicine or *healing nectar* (Skt. *amṛta*) which brings calmness, peace, and the coolness discussed before. It is very beneficial and is like a great and powerful medicine. It just flows out quite spontaneously and naturally from the presence of one's bodhicitta. Take the supreme example of bodhicitta: when the Buddha taught, he led a very simple life and everything happened spontaneously around him. These far-reaching effects were a completely natural outflow of this very therapeutic healing, coming from the very pure motivation which he had. This is very special. If one looks, for instance, at the Catholic church, one can see that it is a very powerful organization and a great deal of effort goes into spreading the doctrine as an organized business. There are missionaries and a definite effort to spread the philosophy and view. Even though there is all that effort and organization, it does not necessarily spread the view of Catholicism. With the Buddhist dharma, in contrast, there is the natural radiance of bodhicitta and the activity of the Buddha which through his very pure mind allows the dharma and its meaning to spread from one person to another in a very spontaneous and natural way.

The two main characteristics of the Buddha's activity are its spontaneity and its eternity. One can see how various cultures of the past such as the Greek civilization influenced the world and one can see how that influence was very short-lived. The activity of Buddha, however, is spreading and increasing all the time without any break in continuity and is always effective wherever it is. The Buddha's activity is also always appropriate and fresh. In the first centuries after the Buddha's passing away, the Buddha's activity was very appropriate. Even 2,000 years later it is still very meaningful and appropriate.

The view or approach of a bodhisattva to the mahāyāna teachings is rooted in the second turning of the wheel of dharma. This second main phase of Buddha's teachings is called "the second turning" or sometimes "the intermediate turning." The first turning was concerned with the four noble truths and was the basis for the hīnayāna. The second turning was the main basis for the mahāyāna. The main topic of the Buddha's teaching in this turning is what is called voidness or emptiness.[11] The Buddha described the empty nature of both outer phenomena of the universe and inner phenomena in the mind of the perceiver. Then later on, in the third turning, the Buddha mainly taught about wisdom (Skt. *jñana*).

When Thrangu Rinpoche was in Germany there was one person who said that he appreciated Rinpoche's teachings very much, but when it came to the teachings on emptiness, they somehow made him feel depressed and uncomfortable. He said that if Rinpoche taught more about the existence of something rather than nonexistence of something, it would probably make him feel better. Because of this discomfort, emptiness will be explained in terms of the simultaneity of emptiness and interdependence called *interdependent origination* (Tib. *tendrel*).

Interdependent Origination

Properly speaking, all phenomena are empty. This emptiness, however, does not mean phenomena are completely nonexistent. It is not a blankness of everything. What it means is that all things depend upon one another for their manifestation because they are interrelated. What we have seen before is that we project a global idea of "I" onto what is in fact many, many different things; so that when we look for the "I" we cannot find it as a thing. We find on closer examination a complete absence of "I," an emptiness of "I." Yet, we can see that in the relative sense because of the way we project this idea, there is a certain relative existence of the "I" in terms of these projections. So, sometimes we associate this idea of self with our body, sometimes with our consciousness, and sometimes we even associate "I" or "mine" with the country that we live in. Therefore, the idea of "I" is related to something, it is based on something, it depends on something like the body or the idea of a country. And yet, when we look for it, we can't find it. It is empty.

When one studies emptiness, one examines how things appear, that is, how an existence which is dependent on one thing or how everything that manifests is interdependent. All the various outer things are related and rest upon one another. Yet, when one looks for the "things" properly and thoroughly, one finds an emptiness; they simply don't exist in those terms.

For instance, if I take a two-inch and a four-inch stick of incense, the four-inch stick is the longer one and the two-inch stick is the shorter one. If I show this to a hundred persons and ask, "Which one is the longer one?" they would all say that the four-inch stick was definitely the longer one. Then when I add a six-inch stick and remove the two-inch stick, the four-inch stick becomes the shorter one. If I ask a hundred people they will all say that the six-inch stick is the longer one and the four-inch stick is the shorter one. So I can't really say this is long or this is short without seeing the interrelationship of the two. There is the relative definition of things and that definition depends on other factors to which the thing is related. Things depend upon one another; they are interdependent; and this is the way all phenomena manifest to us. They don't have a meaning and significance by themselves; their significance emerges because of their relationship to other things.

There is an interdependence of all phenomena. That dependence applies to everything, but this dependence is particularly strong in terms of the labeling and recognizing the mind of the observer. If one takes away the observer with the ideas of long-short or large-small, then things by themselves don't have largeness or smallness. It is only when an observer is present and from this relative point of view decides that this is large, this is small, this is good, this is bad, this is beautiful, this is ugly, etc. Without the observing mind, these characteristics aren't present. So, the pleasantness or unpleasantness of phenomena depend upon the person relating to it. If someone is attached to an object thinking they want it, it becomes a nice and desirable thing. If it is something they don't like, it becomes distasteful, something to get rid of. All of this depends upon the observer's mind; interdependence takes place mainly between the defining mind and the apparent world.

Thus, the way things are defined depends on the individual who is observing and defining. For instance, if two tigers see each other, they find each other quite attractive. They think, "Oh, how nice" when they see each other. However, when a man sees a tiger, he thinks, "Oh, this is terrible!" not "Oh, what an attractive thing." Then the other way around, if two people meet each other they think, "Oh, how nice. That's my friend." Yet when a tiger sees someone, he doesn't think, "Oh, that's nice. It's a human." He thinks, "Yum, food!" So we see from these different relationships that the quality of nice, attractive, food, or frightening is not contained within the object itself, but depends upon who is relating to that object and the way we label, define, and conceive of that object. We tend to label and define everything and we conceive of objects as real even though our concept is based on a relative, dependent process; things just manifest to us and because of this they have reality for us.

It should be obvious that the relative existence of things depends upon the mind of the observer. Because of this the Buddha gave teachings on the simultaneity of emptiness and interdependence and showed how these affect us. Interdependence, relative existence, and emptiness go hand in hand; the two are simultaneous and in combination. As we have seen in the example of the tigers and people, it is not that there is an absolute quality permanently engraved into the object; it is a relative quality that is there because of the observer. Because of interdependence in the relative world, there is this manifestation of these various relative qualities. Yet, when we examine them closely, there is nothing of an absolute value to be found in them. If we look for the absolute quality of beauty, edibility, or as we saw with the sticks, the absolute quality of longness-shortness, bigness-smallness, etc. these qualities cannot be found.

In the relative world, things continue to manifest to us, even though there is absolute emptiness. This means that suffering and all things happen on a relative level. Yet, when we really search, we can never find the suffering, only the emptiness of suffering. So, in our relative life, we have all these various experiences which are interdependent. In this deluded existence we produce the various defilements; sometimes we are attached to things, sometimes we become aggressive towards various people; sometimes we become jealous or proud. The way to overcome these defilements is not to work with the outer phenomena, but to work with the mind which experiences these things. So, for instance, we have an enemy; we can't just get rid of the enemy because, if we were to kill the enemy, then his or her mother, father, brothers or sisters would end up being our enemies. So destroying the outer enemy is not very practical. Whereas if we can work with our mind which relates to that person as an enemy and we can change that relationship to love and compassion and patience with what is taking place, the situation of an enemy is no longer there because the interdependence between us and "enemy" has been changed. To help us learn how to undergo this sort of transformation the Buddha taught the simultaneity of emptiness and interdependence.

Relative and Absolute Truth

One may wonder if realizing the absolute truth doesn't make everyday life and ordinary things meaningless. It does not because when one gains realization into the absolute nature of things, everyday life does not become contradictory in that sense. This is called the realization of the two truths. This means that one studies on the absolute level the way things really are and on the relative level one studies the way things take place according to the strict laws of interdependence. The relative world has its relative truth and the absolute truth also has its truth. If it weren't like that, absolute truth would be called "the truth" and relative truth would be called "lies." But it is called the absolute truth and the relative truth, so it is seeing the way things really are when one looks absolutely or whether one considers the way things seem to manifest.

When we realize both of these truths together, it helps us to live in the relative sense and it is of great practical use. For instance, if someone becomes angry and aggressive towards us, normally we become excited and flare up and fight back. If we realize that what is taking place is a relative and dependent situation, and we are aware of the two truths, then we don't need to strike back. Because we don't strike back, we don't harm ourself through generating negative karma and we don't harm the other person. So the two truths are useful. We can see the two things happening: the relative situation emerging and the value of the ground of absolute truth.

It is the same with desire. Normally we are subject to desire and wanting things. If we can't get them, we become upset thinking, "I must have that. I can't carry on without it." or "I need it." And if we don't get it, our life becomes very miserable. Or if we have something like a precious statue or vase and one day it gets scratched or breaks, we become upset and feel, "Now it is ruined. I loved that thing." However, when we understand relative and absolute truth, we realize there is something useful to be learned if we get it or don't get it and therefore we develop evenness. We don't build a situation of desire or become heart-broken if something gets scratched or spoiled. So understanding the two truths enables us to live very skillfully and once we have that deep realization, then we still go on trying to make the relative world more beneficial. It all becomes like a play or a dream. We are still working to make a beneficial situation, but because there is no longer any grasping or attachment, we work in a more relaxed way.

We may think wanting to practice the dharma is also grasping. But there is a difference between desire and desire for good which is often called "aspiration." In Tibetan these are two different words. Desire (Tib. *chag pa*) means wanting things for oneself. It has the feeling of attachment, involvement, grasping, and self-interest. Aspiration (Tib. *mö pa*) has the meaning of concern with positive things, of helping others, and of seeing what is necessary and wishing to do what is necessary and useful. As our wisdom and insight grows, hopefully, our desires will decrease. Our aspiration will increase because of the increase of wisdom and insight. An example of this might be that we fall asleep and begin to dream of being attacked by a tiger. We are full of fear and if there is someone nearby who is clairvoyant, he or she would see what we are dreaming and would know we were dreaming of a tiger. So the clairvoyant wakes us up and says, "There is no need to be frightened of the tiger. It's just a dream. It is not really there." When we see the true nature of things (absolute truth), our aspiration grows and we want to do what is beneficial and useful. We are like the clairvoyant person and aspire to help relieve the suffering we see in others.

The effect of attachment can be seen in the behavior of couples. If they are not very involved with each other and just like each other, then they can have a sweet and smooth relationship. But when they have great attachment and involvement in each other, then it only takes one of them to go somewhere for a few minutes or to talk to someone else to cause the other partner to ask, "What did you say? What did you do? Where did you go?" One can see that great involvement in the situation causes a lot of difficulties. When one develops wisdom, the involvement decreases and aspiration increases.

At Namo Buddha in Nepal (where Thrangu Rinpoche has his three-year retreat center) the Buddha in a former life gave his body to the tigress and her cubs who were starving. There was a great benefit to him when he saw the tigress and her cubs before him, because at that instant he realized that the thousands and thousands of previous physical lives had not really served much benefit to beings. Each time that he died his body was burned and buried, but it had not been of much use to anyone. He could see that there was the opportunity to actually use the substance of his body for some real benefit, to save lives by feeding the tigress and her cubs. Because he had this blend of compassion and wisdom, he knew that by giving so totally he would develop and perfect the *pāramitā* of generosity and through its karmic power would give tremendous impetus to his development of wisdom in the future. The Buddha could then see not only the immediate benefit of giving himself to the tigress, but also see how this act would bring very great benefit in the future.

Luminosity

The motivation and attitude of the bodhisattva and the mahāyāna practitioner are composed of two main elements: the understanding of emptiness and the understanding of the *dharmadhātu* aspect. These are the main topics of Buddha's second turning of the wheel of dharma. With this view one sees how everything is empty, but at the same time within that emptiness everything takes place infallibly according to the process of interdependence. The second main aspect of the view of the bodhisattva is what is called the "clarity aspect" or "wisdom aspect" or "jñana aspect." This is the main topic of the last turning of the wheel of dharma. This emptiness is not a great blank or voidness. If it were just that, it would be the very opposite of the idea of manifestation. If there is just emptiness, then there can be no manifestation because the two are incompatible with each other. To think of emptiness just in terms of voidness is not correct because emptiness is the non-validity or non-presence of a true thing, a true essence. Nevertheless, through a process of interdependence on a relative level things do manifest: they take place simultaneously with emptiness. So, we can't think of emptiness in terms of just voidness because there is manifestation, yet when we look for the essence of the emptiness, we can't find it. So this emptiness has the nature of *luminosity* or clarity (Tib. *salwa*). The Tibetan word *salwa* is associated with the brightness of sunlight or a very powerful light. Once there is that brightness, everything can be seen and distinguished very clearly. So the nature of emptiness is clarity because it has the ability to let things manifest very precisely from within it. This clarity is synonymous with the wisdom aspect of emptiness because wisdom sees everything clearly. But that wisdom does not have a solid existence; therefore it is not an objective reality that we can feel an aversion or an attraction towards.

The very nature of this wisdom is emptiness. That is why we speak of the union of wisdom and emptiness. When we look at the very essence of emptiness, we find it contains this very wisdom, this clarity, that understands everything. By analyzing that wisdom we discover no objective existence. So its very nature is emptiness; at one and the same time there is wisdom and there is emptiness.

Buddha Nature

The union of wisdom and emptiness is the essence of Buddhahood or what is called *Buddha-nature* (Skt. *tathāgatagarba*) because it contains the very seed, the potential of Buddhahood.[12] It resides in each and every being and because of this essential nature, this heart nature, there is the possibility of reaching Buddhahood. Even though it is in everyone, it is not obvious nor does it manifest because it is covered up by the various thoughts and defilements which are blocking the Buddha-nature.

That Buddha-nature is present in each and every being but does not always manifest. This is exemplified in the *Uttara Tantra* by an image of a lotus flower, which is an ugly flower when it is a bud. But inside it there is a small and perfect Buddha statue. At first one only sees this homely flower. Yet, when the flower blossoms one can see the form of the Buddha, which has always been there. Similarly, full Buddha-nature is in everyone's mind, yet its radiance and presence is covered up.

Another example given in the *Uttara Tantra* is of honey surrounded by many bees. Honey is quite sweet and tasty but as long as it is surrounded by bees, one can't taste that sweetness. The example shows again that there is something at the very heart, yet because of these swarms of bees which represent our defilements, one can't gain access to something which has been there all the time.

The third example is of grains of rice inside their husks. To get the nutritional value from the grains one has to remove the shell, the husk. Whether one dehusks the grain or not, there is always that same grain inside and as far as the grain is concerned there is no difference. But if one wants to have access to the nutritive value, one must remove the shell.

The example of the statue of the Buddha inside the lotus shows how buddha essence is inside beings but is covered up by desires, attachments, and involvements. One has many different defilements. The first main defilement (Skt. *kleśa*) of attachment is represented by the lotus because when one finds something very attractive, one wants to be involved with it. The lotus flower at one stage is very beautiful and has a nice shape and color which is associated with beauty and attractiveness. Actually, when one considers it, the lotus has a very limited use apart from its beauty. Also that beauty changes—one day it very beautiful, the following days it wilts, fades and rots and the beauty is gone. This is the very nature of desire—at one point things seem very attractive but very quickly one realizes that they are not so useful or lasting as they seemed. In the example of the lotus it is not until the petals of the flower open and fall away that one can see the form of the Buddha that was there all the time. And it is the same with desires—until one's desires have been eliminated, one cannot see the Buddha-nature which has been inside sentient beings all the time.

The second example of honey points to the covering or blocking presence of the second defilement of aggression or anger which is characterized by bees. Honey in itself is very sweet and tasty. This is like Buddha-nature which is very useful and beneficial for everyone. Yet, around the honey are all those bees whose nature is the very opposite. The bees sting and are very aggressive. As long as the bees are there, the situation is very difficult. So it is with the nature of aggression and anger which is also very unpleasant; it stings and hurts. The honey is there all the time and one can't get to the honey because the bees are all around it. If one can find a way of gradually getting rid of the bees, one can get the honey. Likewise, when one eliminates anger and aggression, one can develop this really beneficial Buddha-nature.

The third example of grains of rice inside their husks is used to point to the nature of the third main defilement which is ignorance or stupidity. The husk is very tough and difficult to separate from the grain which makes it a good example of ignorance which is also thick, strong, and difficult to get rid of. This ignorance stops us from having access to Buddha-nature.

Generally speaking, beings have a great deal of ignorance. Compared to animals, of course, humans are more clever in many respects and have more wisdom. But the wisdom of humans is quite limited. For instance, humans like ourselves can't see what is happening beyond the walls of this room; they can't see what is happening in the rest of the world. Knowledge stops where the wall stops. Even though humans can see other people inside the walls, they have no idea apart from a few vague indications what's happening inside of people because human perception doesn't stretch that far. Even when we think we perceive other's thoughts, we often make mistakes. If we have a friend, for instance, the friend goes out and we may start thinking, "I wonder what he is saying about me" and we develop a whole train of thought and become convinced that he is saying bad things about us. By the time he comes back there can even be a fight just because we have guessed the person's intentions wrongly. Or we may think an adversary is changing his intentions towards us by acting in an open way which can also cause a lot of trouble if the enemy in fact is still an enemy. It is hard for us to see things as they really are.

When we learn about the Buddha's teachings, we learn about the nature of desire, the nature of aversion, and so on. It takes a long time for us to understand what is really being taught. Even though we may know about the shortcomings of desire, yet due to our habitual patterns it takes a long time to act in a way which corresponds to our knowledge. The perception of the deeper aspects of truth is very hard for us to quickly understand because ignorance is so pervasive. That is why it is compared to the husk of a grain: It is tough, hard, and takes a lot of effort to remove.

These three examples show how Buddha-nature is like a precious essence or jewel inside us, which is covered up by desire, aggression, and ignorance. The Buddha taught the dharma to show us how to have access to this precious Buddha-nature.

There is another example in the *Uttara Tantra* which illustrates this. There's a very precious statue made of gold which ages ago had fallen and became covered with dirt. Because no one knows it's there, for generations and generations people leave their rubbish there and it becomes more and more covered because no one realizes it is underground. One day a man who is clairvoyant comes along and sees this precious golden statue under the ground. He then tells someone, "Do you know that there is a precious and beautiful golden statue there under the ground. All you need to do is dig it up, clean it, and you will own this extremely valuable thing." Someone with sense would heed the man, take the statue out of the ground, clean it, and possess what has been there for such a long time. This example is very vivid: Since the beginning of time this precious Buddha-nature has been in all beings, yet it has been covered with the dirt of the defilements. Because one doesn't realize one has this precious nature within, defilements build up. But then the Buddha who is like the man with clairvoyance tells us, "You know, there is Buddha-nature within you. All you need to do is uncover and clean it so all the exceptional qualities it has will manifest." Those who heed the Buddha's teachings can discover this incomparable thing which has been within us all the time and which we never knew was there until we were told. For that essence to be revealed we need to meditate on the truth, on the essence of phenomena, the way things really are. If we do that, we clean away all the delusions and defilements which have been covering up that essence. So we meditate on the essence of everything which is emptiness. Through that meditation we will discover this emptiness has within it wisdom and clarity. Through the process of becoming used to the emptiness and clarity which is the universal essence or *dharmatā* we will automatically eliminate all of the delusions which have been blocking that vision. Once we see the truth of everything, all the deluded aspects can't exist at the same time. So to clear away the obscurations and blockages to Buddha-nature, we need first to know about the essence of emptiness and clarity. Once we know it exists, we meditate on it to become closer and closer to Buddha-nature.

The Six Pāramitās

The practice of the mahāyāna of the bodhisattva is mainly concerned with the six *pāramitās.* There are in fact ten[13] pāramitās but six of these are most commonly spoken of. So we will discuss the six pāramitās which constitute the bodhisattva's practice.

The Buddha said that when we do dharma practice, it should be done in a genuine and heartfelt way. This means that when we practice dharma, we must not just do it as an outer show or pretense or like a theatrical performance where actors dress up as kings and ministers even though they are not really kings and ministers. We must practice dharma wholeheartedly and very properly with our body, speech, and mind. When we perform virtuous actions with our body, our mind should be there also working for dharma. When we say things, our mind should mean it as well. Practicing the dharma whole-heartedly is very important. If we do a prostration, for instance, our mind should also be filled with faith, devotion, and confidence to make that prostration meaningful. But if we just prostrate with the body and the mind is not involved with it, then it is more like theater with us just going through the movements, but the power is not there. It is the same when we recite *mantras*. If we recite a mantra and at the same time our mind is visualizing, we are filled with certainty, confidence, and faith; then all the power of the mind will be there and it will be a very good practice. But if we just recite the mantras and our mind is elsewhere, then it is just a show and the power is not there. It is not necessarily a bad thing to just do a prostration or a mantra mouthing the words. It just means the power is not there; just as it is not necessarily a bad thing that people pretend to be king and ministers in the theater. So, if we really want to get everything possible out of practice, we need to do it very sincerely and wholeheartedly with our body, speech, and mind.

With this wholehearted approach the bodhisattva's practice is the practice of the six pāramitās. The first is generosity which means giving. There is giving to those who are worse off than oneself such as the poor, needy, and hungry. Then there is giving to those who are better off than oneself which means offering them the three jewels. These are the two main areas of generosity of the bodhisattva. When giving to those who are worse off, what is important is compassion and when giving to those who are better off what is important is faith, devotion, and confidence. So when one gives to the poor, one relieves their poverty and hunger temporarily because of compassion. When one makes offerings to the three jewels, one makes an expression of devotion. If one never gives to those worse off, then compassion isn't there and it is not complete. In the same way, if one doesn't make offerings to the three jewels, then one's faith, confidence and appreciation in the meaning of the three jewels isn't quite right either. So offerings are a very important sign of what is going on in terms of compassion and devotion. Beside cultivating love, compassion, and devotion, the bodhisattva also has to actually practice the pāramitā of generosity.

The second pāramitā is moral or virtuous conduct. The very essence of virtuous conduct is that through love and compassion one does not directly harm other beings. If one has love and compassion and yet harms other beings, it is a sign that one's love and compassion isn't really there. So, if one is loving and compassionate, one must really never harm other beings. This is the bodhisattva's approach to love and compassion. Therefore virtuous conduct is mainly concerned with the discipline of practicing right conduct with one's body and speech so that one doesn't hurt others directly or indirectly.

Generosity and virtuous conduct depend mainly on oneself. If one makes an effort to be loving and compassionate, it is relatively easy to develop generosity. Also, if one is loving and compassionate, it is relatively easy to maintain high moral conduct because this depends mainly on working with oneself.

The third pāramitā deals with something more difficult. It deals with how we react to situations arising from others, particularly what we do in the face of physical and verbal aggression from others. This is the pāramitā of forbearance, often called patience, which is remaining loving and compassionate in the face of aggression. The training of patience is the training of keeping one's love and compassion in the face of those difficulties which come from other people. So if our love and compassion is incredibly stable, when others hit us, no matter how much they hurt us physically, we never reply in a like manner. Our only response is one of love, compassion, and understanding. In order to practice generosity, virtuous conduct, and patience in the face of difficulties, one needs the fourth pāramitā of diligence to implement the first three pāramitās and make them increase and become even more powerful factors in our life.

Diligence doesn't mean some terrible drudge or difficult effort. Rather it is very joyful, meaningful, and vital. If one really thinks something has benefit, one values it, and one will do it very joyfully and out of this there is an automatic flow of diligence and industry. If one thinks something is not very important, then one will think it is a drag and a bore and one will do a little bit and then become lazy and stop. Later one may try to do a little bit more and stop again because of laziness.

Diligence means to practice without falling under the influence of laziness and practicing because one realizes the tremendous value of that practice. Once one has gained an insight into its value, effortlessly there will be joy and keenness to get on with it. Then automatically one will put lots and lots of effort into it to make it a very productive thing. One will become diligent thus increasing the preceding pāramitās.

The fifth pāramitā is mental stability. The Tibetan word for this pāramitā is *gom* which is the word for "to meditate." This is the active word and the word is derived from the root (Tib. *khom*) which means "to accustom oneself to something." So to meditate means to commit and to accustom oneself to meditation. It really means to train to settle. Even though we say "my mind," the mind which belongs to us is not under our control. Because we have not worked on it very much, our mind tends to be very distracted; it switches from one thing to another all the time. For instance, we may decide, "I am not going to get angry anymore." Even though we decide that in one moment, we don't have control over our mind and so we fall under the influence of anger a little later. We may promise not to be subject to desires any more and then we lose control and our mind is suddenly full of desires. So, we think "my mind is under my control," but when we look at it carefully there is not that much control there. It is not like our hand. If we want the hand to go somewhere, we can put it there. If we want it to come back, we can bring it back. But the mind is not nearly so tamed and doesn't respond to those commands so well. This is mainly because we haven't really done much work in bringing it under control. The word "meditation" has this implication of training or habituating our mind so that it does what we want. We habituate our mind by meditating again and again. This is the nature of meditation and the main point of the fifth pāramitā, mental stability.

The sixth pāramitā is wisdom or prajña in Sanskrit. How much happiness we get out of worldly things depends on how much understanding and wisdom we have. So wisdom is the very root of happiness and joy and determines the value of all other things. In the ultimate sense the benefit that we can get depends very much on our wisdom and understanding. Also the ability to help others depends on the degree of our wisdom. Developing ourself also depends on the degree to which we have cultivated wisdom. For all these reasons wisdom and understanding are the very root of happiness and out of them joy emerges. How then does one cultivate this wisdom? For a Buddhist it is cultivated by the three main approaches of studying, contemplating, and meditating.

The Three Approaches to the Path

The first is studying, an act which does not have direct access to wisdom. We don't naturally know how to help wisdom develop, so we turn to the teachings of the Buddha. By studying the teachings, we begin to grasp the ways to the development of wisdom. Now study in itself will not bring the growth of much wisdom. We need to go on to the second step which is contemplation of the teachings in which we think again and again about the meaning of what we have studied to really get to the heart of it. Even this won't bring about the highest, deepest, or ultimate benefit; we need to take the third approach which is to meditate. It is through meditation that we actually attain the ultimate emergence of wisdom. Of the three main modes of developing wisdom, by far the most important one is the wisdom that emerges from our meditation.

All beings have already within them Buddha-nature or this buddha potential which has the essence of clarity and wisdom. This is the very highest wisdom, the power to know everything very clearly and directly. All the power of wisdom is already there, but it is still obscured. Until we have purified the obscurations covering it, we can't use that wisdom because we don't have access to the great clarity within us. We see this even when we try to analyze a simple object. Between us and the thing we are trying to understand there is this intermediate space full of thoughts. We interact with things through a great layer of intellectual activity or subtle subconscious thoughts. It is therefore very hard to actually know something directly because this constant interference of thought takes place. If we study for even a few minutes a great number of thoughts just pop up in our mind. From this we can begin to understand what an obstacle thoughts present to our actual development and understanding.

When we meditate, the purpose of meditation is for our mind to become stable and no longer distracted by the influence of thoughts. Our mind becomes calm and under control. Once the mind is calm, we can have a much more direct and immediate contact with reality and develop wisdom more rapidly. This is why the wisdom which develops in meditation is important.

The Fruition

So far we have examined the view, the meditation, and the practice in the mahāyāna. Now we will move on to fruition which is Buddhahood. The word for "Buddha" in Tibetan has two syllables, *sang gay*. These show the two main qualities or principle aspects of this highest goal of Buddhahood. The first is the aspect of purity which means one is free from all the impurities of the defilements, from ignorance, and from all the obscurations. The syllable *sang* means "awakened," "awakened from that sleep of ignorance," or "purified from that ignorance." The second syllable *gay* means "blossomed" because being free from impurities, all of the deep wisdom of the Buddha becomes present and this clarity and knowledge has completely blossomed and is completely free from obscurations. So Buddhahood is the complete blossoming of the highest wisdom and purity.

The teachings of the Buddha can be divided into three main levels or yānas which are the hīnayāna, the mahāyāna, and the vajrayāna. Another way of analyzing them is to look at them in terms of the *sūtra* and the *tantra* level of teaching. The Sanskrit word sūtra was translated into Tibetan as *do* which means "teachings" or "explanation." Generally, the sūtra level of teachings contains all of the explanations, all the ways of presenting the vast meaning that the Buddha gave in his life of teachings. So the sūtra tradition is a way of presentation of the Buddha's teachings.

The other aspect is the tantra. When this Sanskrit word was translated into Tibetan, it became *gyu* which means "continuum." Sometimes it is called *mantra* which in Tibetan is *nga*. This word "continuum" shows that there is this presence of Buddha-nature or Buddha-essence in all sentient beings that they had have from the very beginning of existence and will possess until they reach Buddhahood. So, by gradually working on the path, step by step, one develops one's full potential and reaches Buddhahood. This constant or continuous presence within us is what is worked with in the tantric teachings. These are teachings related to the vajrayāna which will be discussed next.

The Third Vehicle of Buddhist Practice

The Vajrayāna

Dorje tekpa

by

Thrangu Rinpoche

Chapter 3

The Vajrayāna

The word *vajra* means "immutability" or "indestructibility." On the relative level there are all the samsaric phenomena which are impermanent and change from one thing into another. On the absolute level the essence is always there and never changes and is not affected by one's relative viewpoint. The main concern of the tantric teachings then is working on this changeless, immutable essence. That is why it is called the vajrayāna or "the vehicle of the changeless."

There are two vehicles: the *sūtrayāna* and the vajrayāna. The sūtrayāna or the "sūtra vehicle" is more related to cause, than result. It is called "the cause which is the vehicle with characteristics" because by developing this sūtra level, one learns all that is necessary to create the conditions to achieve the effect or result. The actual result is the vajrayāna. To attain the result, one needs to train in the sūtrayāna. The sūtras show the nature of phenomena. They show what is virtuous and what is not; they show the value of practicing certain things and giving up other things, they show the nature of cause and effect (karma), and what one is trying to develop and what one is trying to eliminate in meditation. We need to train in the sūtras first to become very clear about how the relative level works. So that is why it is called "the causal condition with characteristics." Sometimes it is also called "the vast aspect" of practice because it touches upon so many different things.

The sūtras are mainly concerned with the development of the various causal conditions for realization. In the tantric approach, one goes directly to the very elements that bring results in one's practice. This result aspect is called the "vajrayāna" or "the quintessential mantra."

The problem with the word "tantra" is that it is not only used by Buddhists but also by Hindus. Apart from having the same name, there is little correspondence between the Buddhist and Hindu tantra except that both have their origins in India and used the Sanskrit language. In many Western books there is a tendency to suggest that the Buddhist tantra is related to Hindu tantra. There are, however, no similarities in philosophy, in practice, in point of view, in origin, or in teachers.So Buddhism and Hinduism are different. The Hindu tantra, for instance, is based on the idea of an *atma* or a "soul" or a "higher self." One practices various yogic meditations using subtle channels, energies, and drops[14] (Skt. *nādī, bindu, and prāṇa*) with the idea of relating them to the atma. The Buddhist philosophy, whether on the sūtra or tantra level, involves trying to understand the absence of self or higher self. So from the beginning these two approaches are very different.

When the dharma teachings went to Tibet, there was the simultaneous development of the sūtra and the tantra approach. The sūtras were studied mainly as a way to understand basic dharma. The tantras were applied principally as a way of meditating. So first one would study the sūtras to find out the way that things were and gain a conviction in the meaning of Buddha's teachings gaining a sound theoretical basis in them. When it came to actually meditating, there was a great emphasis on the tantra or vajrayāna techniques in Tibet. So in Tibet there was the sūtrayāna level of meditation called *je gom* which is usually translated as "analytical meditation" in which one gradually works through the analysis of various phenomena understanding the various objects of meditation, and develops wisdom, which emerges through analysis. The meditation related to the vajrayāna is called *jo gom* which is usually translated as "placement meditation" or "direct abiding meditation." In this meditation one concentrates not on the analysis of external objects, but goes directly to resting deeply in the inner mind, and by doing this, one quickly experiences the deeper aspects of meditation.

The reason the vajrayāna was favored in Tibet was that it causes a much more rapid and direct way of reaching the goal of enlightenment. The analytical sūtrayāna approach tends to take much more time although both approaches lead to the same result. Analytical meditation is mainly based on the development of wisdom. Vajrayāna meditation is mainly based on faith and confidence. To develop sūtrayāna meditation one needs wisdom; to gain the results of vajrayāna meditation one needs faith. Generally, the sūtrayāna was studied at the same time that one was meditating on the vajrayāna level so these two methods could reinforce each other. If a person follows purely the sūtrayāna approach, the ordinary mahāyāna can take a long time. For example, to develop the pāramitā of generosity one must develop one's generosity to such a point that one would give up even one's arms, legs, or even the whole body. The cultivation of all these pāramitās is a very large task. Compared to this, the vajrayāna is a more simple and easy task. When properly practiced, it enables one to achieve the goal of Buddhahood through *skillful means* in a single lifetime.

The vajrayāna has several names. Sometimes it is called in Tibetan *dorje tegpa* or "the vajrayāna" where *dorje* is "vajra" and *tegpa* is "yāna." Another word used for the vajrayāna is the Tibetan word *sang gnak* which is often inappropriately translated as the "secret mantrayāna." The actual meaning of the Tibetan syllable *gnak* or "mantra" here is being able to achieve the goal very quickly or quickly getting the results one wants. The syllable *sang* in the word is sometimes translated as "secret," but it really means "very vital" or something which is "quintessential" or "necessary and vital." For example, a machine has many vital parts which allow it to work. These parts are called the *sang* in Tibetan meaning the very core, or the very essence of the machine. So *dorje tegpa* actually means a very "indestructible vehicle" which contains the vital thing which enables one to reach the goal very quickly. When this word is translated as "secret" it gives the incorrect impression of something which needs to be covered up. This is incorrect because the word *sang gnak* doesn't mean "a secret," but it means "the vital essence."

The Importance of the Guru

In the vajrayāna the skillful means to achieve the goal is divided into the creation stage (Tib. *che rim*) and the completion stage (Tib. *dzo rim*) of meditation. In the creation stage we are learning how to transform our perception into pure appearances. To achieve this purity, we meditate basically on the three roots. These are the *gurus* who are the root of the blessings and the transmission of abilities, the *yidams* who are the root of the spiritual powers (*siddhis*), and the protectors who are the ḍākas and ḍākinīs who are the source of all activities to be accomplished. By meditating on these, we are able to touch the level of the pure dimension in our meditation. In the vajrayāna path our wishes are very immediate. When we try to attain the blessing or the power of realization, we find the source of that blessing is the Buddha. But the Buddha lived 2,500 years ago so it's hard to have much confidence that the blessing will cover such a distance in time between us and the Buddha. Nevertheless, this is not important because our own root guru and the gurus of the lineage have this very same blessing, this power of dharma, in exactly the same amount as the Buddha. The Buddha transmitted this power of realization or blessing to his students. They perfected it and it has been handed down absolutely perfectly and unspoiled to the present day so there is absolutely no difference between receiving it from them and having received it 2,500 years ago from the Buddha. This is the gift of the gurus of the lineage. We receive this by opening ourselves to the blessings and transmissions through *guru yoga* practice to the gurus of the lineage.

To be open enough to receive the blessings and transmissions, we need to do guru yoga practice and to think of our guru as being exactly the same as the Buddha. Even more than that, if we think he or she is even better than the Buddha, we will be able to receive the fullness of the dharma and the blessing it contains. It might not be apparent that our guru is identical to the Buddha. But the guru has all the transmissions and by receiving the essence of the teachings from the guru, we will be able to develop the practices just as if we had studied with the Buddha himself. So there is no difference between studying under our own guru or studying with the Buddha. The guru is even better than the Buddha. We are not able to make a connection with the historical Buddha by meeting him but we are able to establish this connection with our own guru. In the vajrayāna we really need to believe that our guru is exactly the same as the Buddha and if we believe that, we can open ourselves enough to receive all of the guru's teachings. If we don't have that confidence, then we are going to doubt the guru's abilities and once we doubt these teachings, we can't put them into practice. If we can't put them into practice, we can't get the full results from them.

The root guru and the gurus of the lineage are the source of the blessing or the transmission of realization. The most important thing in receiving these blessings is our faith, devotion, and confidence in the gurus and their teachings. For example, imagine that there is a very large sparkling diamond. Just seeing it immediately starts us thinking about how we can get it. We really want it and appreciate it and will work very hard and do lots of things to obtain it. If it were, however, just brass or copper, we are not going to strive to get it in the same way. If it were just trash, rather than striving for it, we will try to get rid of it. So how we relate to something, how much we want to have it, depends on our attitude towards it. So the vital teachings and transmissions the guru holds are valuable only if we have great faith, confidence, and devotion. With these we will work hard to develop them.

Meditation on Yidams

When we do guru yoga we meditate on those gurus in an outer[15] way to gain this blessing. Actually the word for "blessing" in Tibetan is *jin lap*. It has the meaning of "the power of dharma," which gives insight, the idea of the very pith or potency of dharma. So this word for "blessing" has the meaning of a "transmission" of dharma. The source of that transmission or power comes from the guru and we meditate on the guru through guru yoga. In particular, Kagyus meditate on Marpa, Milarepa, Gampopa and the Karmapas.[16] They meditate on them externally to gain this closeness and receive this blessing or transmission from them.

We also meditate on the yidams who are the source of our accomplishment. The word "accomplishment" is *siddhi* in Sanskrit and *ngö drub* in Tibetan. The Tibetan *ngö drub* means to "actually complete something." What we accomplish is the fruition of our dharma practice. In the vajrayāna there are two kinds of accomplishment: the general and the supreme accomplishment. The supreme accomplishment is the achievement of Buddhahood by meditating on the yidam.

On the path we progress from stage to stage and develop the miraculous powers and the very deep transcendent insights which come from the yidam. This general accomplishment comes from the development of dharma. In the beginning we study the dharma. In the intermediate phase we reflect very deeply and develop a much deeper understanding of what we have studied. Eventually, through meditation, we enter into the real heart or pith of the meaning of dharma. It is through this process of the development of dharma that Buddhahood emerges. In this way, all the general and extraordinary accomplishments emerge.

The dharma is vast because the Buddha taught 84,000 aspects of dharma. It would be difficult to master all of these. Fortunately, we don't need to master all 84,000 aspects to attain Buddhahood. In fact, just fully mastering one aspect of what Buddha taught will lead to Buddhahood. We can practice meditation on a yidam and gain Buddhahood. Yidam practice is a very powerful practice that combines the essence of the dharma. So if we properly do the creation stage and the completion stage of meditation on a particular yidam, we can traverse the whole path of dharma and gain all its benefits.

The Tibetan word *yidam* means "to commit oneself" or "to set one's mind on something." The syllable *yi* means "mind" and the syllable *dam* means "to commit." So in yidam practice one becomes determined to meditate on one of these yidams and to follow this practice all the way through until the attainment of enlightenment. So one vows, "through this yidam practice I will attain the very highest state, the supreme accomplishment of Buddhahood." One sets one's mind very determinedly on the decision to gain all the beneficial powers by the practice of yidam meditation. These yidams are the transcendental aspects of one's mind's commitment so this is what yidam deities lead us to see.

There are many different forms of yidams. There are yidams associated in particular with the development of skillful means—the male aspect—and yidams in particular associated with the development of wisdom—the female aspect. There are yidams which are peaceful in their appearance that help develop peace and great calmness. Then there are yidams which are wrathful which help develop the dynamism of activity in order to accomplish all the good activities one wishes to do. There are yidams of different colors related to the kind of activity that one wants to develop. For instance, for peaceful activity, there is a white yidam such as Chenresig which is a male form of the yidam. Jetsun Drolma (Skt. Tārā), however, is a female form of peaceful activity. Dorje Sempa (Skt. Vajrasattva) is an example of the peaceful form while Dorje Palmo (Skt. Vajrayoginī) is an example of the wrathful form. So there are many, many different forms and appearances of the yidam. There are so many different forms because the practitioner's aspirations and abilities are so very different from one another that one yidam doesn't suit everyone. So these yidams correspond to the various needs of the different students at various stages of practice.

Most people have an impure perception. We therefore meditate on yidams to help eliminate the various impure mental habits and conditioning that we have built up over many lifetimes. We meditate on the yidams in the creation stage to carry out this purification. So in yidam practice there is the stage of disassociating ourselves mentally from impure images by letting our awareness dissolve into emptiness. From that emptiness we begin to associate with the yidam who is the manifestation of the pure qualities. So through meditation on the yidam, we condition ourselves to purity and help free ourselves from our impure conditioning.

The concepts of birth and death (that is, arising, generation, and dissolution) are purified by meditation on the yidam. In the initial stage of meditation we let everything dissolve into emptiness to purify our concepts of death. For birth, we meditate, for example, on the emergence from emptiness of the seed syllable of TAM and then meditate on the gradual emergence of the various details of visualization. This purifies the various ideas and concepts of birth. We also have ideas about our own inferiority and this great tendency holds us back. To purify this hesitancy, we meditate on the yidam in space so the *jñānasattva* aspect, the wisdom aspect charged with the real presence, materializes in space before us. We identify with that jñāna aspect to overcome this identification with the weak or inferior side of our nature.

There are many different styles of meditating on the yidams. Sometimes we visualize them above our head. Sometimes we visualize that we have become completely transformed into their form. And sometimes we visualize them in space in front of us. Generally speaking, there are many different styles of visualization because there are different needs, aspirations, and stages of development of meditators. Even though there are many different ways of meditating on the yidams, the dominant way of visualizing the yidam is to visualize oneself as being transformed into the yidam. This eliminates previous impure conditioning and helps us to learn how to relate to the purity that the yidams represent. For example, we visualize a peaceful yidam as being extremely beautiful and inspiring and adorned with beautiful clothes and precious ornaments and so on. In the same way, we visualize wrathful yidams as really terrifying. If we only pretend to visualize, it becomes fabricated and we don't get the full benefit of the practice. Whereas, if we meditate with great conviction, relating to and identifying with these various forms; this will actually bring about a change in our meditation developing it and making it much more stable.

There are many reasons why one meditates on yidams. One identifies with these pure forms to free oneself from the conditioning and impurity which has been built up in the past. One visualizes the real presence of the deity to develop confidence in the existence of this purity. If one practices *śamatha* meditation by itself, one finds it quite difficult to attain peace and insight without a lot of effort. However, visualizing and identifying with the yidams is a very useful way of developing one's śamatha meditation. If one just tries to rest one's mind, it is very hard to calm it down. Whereas if one tries to visualize the appearance, the face, the hands, the clothing of the yidams, one finds it is easier to do. Through accustoming oneself to yidam meditation, the power of śamatha meditation will develop quite quickly.

With all meditation if one is too tense and tries too hard, one won't achieve very much. On the other extreme, if one is too relaxed, one won't receive much benefit either. This is also true with yidam meditation. If one is too tense, one won't be able to visualize very clearly in the creation stage. If one is too relaxed, the yidam won't appear either. However, with the development of one's power to visualize a deity, one's śamatha meditation will increase. They help each other: śamatha meditation helps the visualization and the visualization helps the śamatha. Also in the different stages of yidam meditation there is usually a period of time when one just rests in the peace of śamatha meditation.

When doing yidam practice, one usually recites a mantra. Sometimes one recites the mantra at the same time as visualizing the yidam and sometimes one just recites the mantra, and at other times one just rests in meditation. There are various ways of doing yidam practice but the overall idea is to employ the body, speech, and mind at the same time. With the body one sits properly; for speech one recites the mantra, and with mind one visualizes the deity or rests in placement meditation. It is beneficial, incidentally, to do the mantra recitation because even the sound of the actual mantra supports the development of meditation. It has its own power. Great benefit also comes to the mind and the development of one's power of absorption by meditating in the creation stage of yidam practice. The actual methods for doing these practices are explained in the instructions for practicing the *sadhānas* such as the Medicine Buddha sadhāna, the Jetsun Drolma sadhāna, or the Chenresig sadhāna. The main idea is that the yidams are the root of the accomplishment of dharma.

The Saṅgha and Protectors

Generally speaking, our friends and helpers on the path of dharma are the saṅgha. The saṅgha are our friends because they tell us of the good qualities we can develop and show us what obstacles might arise and how to avoid them. They can even help us foresee the obstacles which may arise and help us steer clear of them. They also give us support and guidance in the areas of increasing beneficial activities and eliminating harmful activities. In the past there have been many Buddhas and bodhisattvas who have been very great friends of beings. Meditating on the protectors in the creation stage of meditation is a way of connecting with their power which helps us remove the various difficulties within and without us. So we pray to them for their help and that help materializes through the *jñānasattva* or wisdom aspect. These Buddhas and bodhisattvas appear in the form of the various dharma protectors. They are called dharma protectors (Skt. *dharmapāla*) and we should never make the mistake of thinking that they are our personal protectors. We should not relate to them to increase our personal interests or to harm other people. The dharma protectors serve entirely to increase all favorable conditions for our dharma practice and to help us remove the various obstacles which can arise in our dharma practice. It is very important that we really believe that they are really there and that we have confidence in their power to help. If we do not have this complete confidence, we will receive little benefit from them. The protectors can remove the obstacles; they can really help us achieve our dharma goals. In vajrayāna practices we can make offerings of *torma* to the protectors and this helps increase our confidence in the protector's help. If we do these things properly and have great faith and confidence in their helping power, the help will really materialize and we will benefit from it. In this way the protectors are the root of activity in the dharma.

The Completion Stage of Meditation

Meditation in the vajrayāna is divided mainly into the creation stage and the completion stage. Previously, the creation stage or the visualizing stage of practice was discussed. Now the completion stage of vajrayāna meditation will be discussed.

The main focus in vajrayāna meditation is working with our mind. It is said that what manifests, what appears to us, is the mind. If we can understand this, we can understand how even the things in the external world—trees, mountains, rocks, flowers, etc.—are creations and experiences of the mind. If we can analyze this carefully enough, we can understand this. Whether these external things are or are not the projections or creations of the mind is not too important because happiness, suffering, and our relationships with the world are very definitely related to our mind. Whether we are attached to things or whether we are repelled by things depends on our mind. Whether we are enjoying what is taking place or not depends on our mind. That's obvious. If two people see the same movie, for example, one may think it is the greatest movie ever made and the other the worst. The movie obviously is the same, but how we feel depends upon our mind. All of our relationships are determined by our mind and our attitude. Also all the defilements and all the products of these defilements are rooted in our mind. Also, all the good qualities of the path emerge from what we do with our mind. For this reason we work principally on the mind in the vajrayāna.

The Four Preliminary Practices

Besides tranquility (Skt. *śamatha*) and insight (Skt. *vipaśyanā*) meditation there are the four ordinary foundations or preliminaries. It is said that the foundations are even more profound than the actual practice itself and the amount of benefit and development that emerges in the main practices is related entirely to how well one has prepared oneself through the foundations. There are two kinds of foundations: the *four ordinary foundations*[17] or four thoughts that turn the mind and the four special foundations or the *four preliminary practices*. These foundations are designed to orient the mind totally towards practice and to ensure that one will later practice with the greatest diligence and enthusiasm. For this reason the foundations, which are the steering force of the practice, are said to be even more important than the actual practice itself.

Meditating Directly on Mind

There are two traditions of tranquility meditation: the sūtra approach which contains the very vast dharma teachings and the tantra approach which contains a profound approach. At the level of the sūtra teachings we learn to understand all the projections and creations of our mind. These vast teachings teach us how to understand and establish the view that the external world of phenomena and internal world of mind are empty. We understand the philosophy of emptiness through these teachings.

The profound approach of the vajrayāna is not so much concerned with establishing the relationship between outer world and inner mind. Instead the main focus in the vajrayāna is working directly on the mind.[18] Whether outer phenomena are projections or not projections or whether the outer world is empty or not empty is not so important at this stage. When one works with mind, one is trying to discover the very essence, the very nature of mind. When one is progressing towards enlightenment, one is not creating new qualities in the mind or taking the mind from one stage to another. Rather one is discovering its true nature which has been invisible because it is clouded by delusions created by mistaken perceptions. So the whole point is to cast aside mistaken perceptions and discover the actual nature of what is already there.

The reason the vajrayāna teachings are called "that which explains directly" or "that which points to meditation" or "that which points to mind itself" is that these teachings are concerned with showing how to meditate and uncover the inner mind. The example that is often employed to demonstrate this process is the example of the rope that is mistaken for a snake. When one sees a rope in a dark room and mistakes it for a snake, one has a sudden fear and panic because of ignorance, delusion, and a mistaken perception. The most useful thing to do in this case is not to create anything new or jump at some new remedy to eliminate the "snake," but to simply realize that the "snake" is actually a rope. Once one sees that it is just a rope, all the fear and delusions automatically disappear. There is no need to do anything about the delusions once the actual nature of what is there is realized.

Similarly, when one does vajrayāna meditation on the actual nature of things, one is not so much concerned with fabricating something or being concerned with various outer delusions. One tries instead to find the very nature of what is there. The mind is turned inward to consider how it is operating. It is the mind which looks at the mind itself. Through this one begins to understand the very nature of the mind and one tastes the very essence of how the mind becomes deluded and lost in various phenomena.

It is important to know how to actually meditate on the essence of mind. The actual essence, the deepest nature of the mind, is dharmadhātu, the empty aspect. Besides dharmadhātu there is the aspect of clarity, the essence of Buddhahood and wisdom, which is also part of the very nature of the mind. This is the true nature of the mind that is eventually discovered. In the beginning we cannot see its nature directly and its nature is not at all evident. When first examining the mind for its nature, we come to the conclusion that the mind is constantly in the throes of wanting and not wanting, of being happy and unhappy. The relationship between this first look at the mind and the true nature of the mind is the relationship between something which is very changeable or fleeting and something which is deeper and more lasting. When the mind is in the throes of happiness and sadness, wanting and rejecting, it is like water that is very agitated, full of mud, and very stirred up. When we examine it, we only see the agitation, the cloudiness, and the dirtiness. However, if we let the water settle without agitating it, the very nature of that water which is clear and calm emerges. If left alone, it settles to become clear and calm. So when the mind is stirred up by these fleeting and changing thoughts of desire and emotion, it is not very clear. It is very turgid. But if we can clear away the dirtiness and agitation, the actual nature of the mind is very lucid and transparent and calm and very peaceful.

The Body in Meditation

One meditates so that one can actually perceive the essence of mind. The essence is constantly there, whether one is walking, sitting, sleeping, and whether one is deluded or not deluded. One could theoretically meditate on the mind on all occasions, but for beginners that is not at all easy. To help beginners eventually become more fully aware of this essence, it is extremely important to set one's body in a good posture while meditating and to learn to control one's mind. Through this one will eventually be able to perceive the essence of mind.

There are the five or seven points of posture for the body and five main points of mental stability for the mind to observe. One should be neither too tense nor too relaxed so one will eventually be able to follow a path which leads to the perception of that essence. When one meditates, one sits very erect and properly. When one's body is straight, the different channels in one's body will also be straight. When the channels are straight, then the energies which move through these channels also move in unobstructed lines. When these energies move correctly, the mind becomes much more stable.

There are five main points of meditation in relation to posture. Firstly we keep the spine straight. This actually is a way to relax and bring well-being into our meditation. If the back is bent by leaning backwards or slanting to the right, left, or forward, we have to make an effort to maintain it and it's not so easy to be relaxed. If the spine is straight, then we don't have to expend effort and meditation becomes naturally comfortable accompanied by a state of well-being.

Secondly, we have the legs crossed when we meditate. Were we to meditate standing up, it would be quite uncomfortable. Were we to meditate lying down, we would become too sluggish. Sitting crosslegged, however, keeps the mind and meditation very stable making a very comfortable and lasting position. That's why we sit crosslegged.

Third, the hands are placed on top of each other in the lap. If the arms were outstretched in all sorts of funny positions, this would give rise to many kinds of feelings and not be very comfortable. Just letting the hands rest in the meditation posture with the palms on top of each other is very relaxed and this doesn't give rise to various feelings.

The fourth point concerns the breath. The breath should not be artificial. Artificial breathing requires effort and making this effort never allows the mind to rest in stability. For that reason we relax, letting the breath be natural, letting it come and go without any effort.

The fifth point is where we look with our eyes. Our mind and thoughts tend to change a lot. This is related to the eyes so that what we do with our eyes is quite important. There are different ways of meditating. The *tirthikas* (the non-Buddhists or Hindus) believe that Indra, Brahma, and the gods are in the heavens and they will often look upwards in meditation. In the Buddhist system, the hīnayāna practitioners will most often meditate with the eyes looking downward because if one looks around one, the objects in view give rise to feelings which are usually associated with the defilements. So they look downward in order not to be aware of these things.

In the vajrayāna we look neither up nor down or away from things, but look straight ahead. If the eyes are tightly closed, we get a sense of darkness as being in a dark room but this doesn't allow much clarity of mind. If, on the other hand, the eyes are too widely open and staring, it is very uncomfortable and takes a lot of effort to maintain. So the eyes are naturally opened; not too closed, not too wide open and looking straight forward. No matter what appears within the field of vision, we meditate with a relaxed mind and don't follow after the various impressions which go through our consciousness. No matter what visual impressions manifest, we don't bother with them because the mind is very relaxed and not conditioned by visual impressions.

The Mind in Meditation

Once we have learned to sit correctly and place the body correctly, we go on to stabilize the mind. Since the main qualities of meditation are dependent upon the connection we have with our guru, the first thing we do is to consider the guru as the very essence of all the buddhas, all the gurus of the lineage, and the transmission of the lineage. The guru is the very essence of all these beings condensed into just one person. To do this we visualize our own guru in the form of Buddha Vajradhara (Tib. Dorje Chang) and visualize him or her above our head or in space before us. It makes no difference whether Vajradhara is visualized in space before us or on top of our head. We meditate on the fact that the guru's presence is the essence of all the gurus and that the form is that of Buddha Vajradhara. We meditate and pray to the guru one-pointedly and at the end we visualize the guru melting into light and this light is absorbed into ourselves. Through the fusion of the guru and ourself, a connection is made in which we obtain both the blessing or the transmission of the essence of the dharma and the seed of accomplishment.

When we have done that, we rest our mind in a completely unfabricated state. First of all, we don't bother remembering things from the past. This means we don't think that yesterday, last month, or last year we did such and such and we don't bother to recall what it was like when we were young. We don't think, "Oh, this person said that" or "I've had this sort of feeling" or "This happened to me." We simply don't bother about our memories and all the data from the past. So when we sit down to meditate we think, "Now I am going to meditate," and we decide positively not to be carried away with thoughts and memories.

We also don't think about the future. Many people worry a bit and feel quite uncomfortable when they receive this instruction and ask, "If I don't think about the future, it is going to be really difficult to make any plans and work out what I am going to do." They have not quite understood that there are two stages in our practice. There is meditation and postmeditation. These instructions of not remembering and not planning are concerned with what we do only when we are actually practicing meditation. In between these periods it is quite all right to plan and work out what to do in relative existence. So, if we are thinking, "I'm going to build a house" or "I'm going to write a letter" or something like that, then the postmeditation phase is the time to sort all this out. If we are full of such thoughts while meditating, the presence of these thoughts and the agitation it creates will prevent us from getting a taste for meditation and developing our meditation further.

So far the obvious level of remembering the past and planning for the future has been explained. But there is also a more subtle level. "Not remembering" means not toying with or chewing over the thoughts which have just occurred or thinking of things which have just happened in previous instances of meditation. We don't think, "Oh, I just thought this" or "This idea just came up" and then begin to contemplate these thoughts. We just leave the mind very relaxed. No matter what thoughts, concepts, or ideas come up we don't bother to consider or analyze them. On the more subtle level of planning the future we don't hope for an experience in meditation and think, "Now I am meditating. This sort of experience will come." Once again we just leave the mind very relaxed without planning, hoping, or contriving the meditation. Even in the present time we don't think, "Now I am meditating and now I am having a thought," and so on.

The reason we don't become involved with thoughts is that if we do pay attention to them, we become involved in a never-ending process of tracing thoughts with "Oh, now I am thinking this. Now I am thinking that thought. Now this thought is occurring. Oh, yes, this thought is nice." This constant recording of what is taking place will go on and on and we will be caught up in the flow of constant observation of what is happening in the mind. That is why we should leave the thoughts completely alone and not pay any attention to them.

It is not good to think of the future on a subtle level. Trying too hard to contrive meditation by thinking, "Oh, now I am thinking this and it ought to be like that," or "Oh, now I am meditating well and must keep it up," or "This isn't so good. I must adjust it so its more like that." is not a useful thing. The Buddha said that if one tries too hard and tries to fabricate the meditation too much, this actually becomes a distraction which troubles the mind. With distraction one never develops stability of mind. For example, if one keeps stirring muddy water, it never becomes clear. The water becomes clear by just leaving it. One can't make the clarity by stirring or doing something to it. One needs to leave it alone to be calm. There's a quotation which says,

If one doesn't trouble the water, it is clear.
If one doesn't fabricate the mind, then it is content.

Our mind's experience is a succession of instants. One instant follows another like a rosary; mental activity is a succession of different experiences one after another. In those instants thoughts can arise or not arise. In meditation when one relaxes in the actual instant without confusing it with the instant that has passed or a future one, there is only the freshness of the moment. One does this without the idea of "this is such and such a thought." One may think that this will create a state of annihilation in the mind. But it doesn't and if one can rest in that freshness, it leads to great clarity. So in the first instant one rests in the freshness and then, without any analysis, one rests in the second instant; whatever is there is also completely fresh and so on. If one can manage to stay within the present instant relaxed and fresh, then great peace and tranquility of mind will automatically emerge. If one is tense or thinking, "Oh, now I have this thought. I must change it," or "I am meditating" then one is not in relaxed meditation. The thing to do is to be relaxed in the freshness of the moment. While being relaxed, one is very attentive with mindfulness and awareness. It means one is aware and mindful of what is happening in a very bright and alert way, like a very good spy. A good spy knows what he is doing, that he is writing a letter now and then is going to go there and so on. So one has this relaxed but incredibly alert mindfulness while being in the freshness of the present moment.

When we meditate, we actually practice both aspects of relaxation in meditation: mindfulness and awareness. When meditation is very comfortable and we aren't troubled by many thoughts, we can just relax in the freshness of the moment. If many thoughts and distractions arise, that is the time to be very mindful and aware of what is taking place. Because of an incredible awareness and sharpness of mind, the thoughts will eventually subside and clarity of mind will increase. So, when a large number of thoughts subside through our alertness and awareness and we become very comfortable, then we can turn down the sharpness and awareness and be more relaxed. Relaxed, however, doesn't mean being carried away by our thoughts because that would be the same as not meditating. Relaxed means to be comfortable in this freshness of this instant of the present time.

At first we do short periods of meditation to be very relaxed in the freshness of the present and try to be very alert about what is taking place. That very alertness doesn't mean one sees the thoughts and thinks, "Oh, these thoughts are a bad thing." It is said that this clarity of mind is unbroken; it is there continuously. By meditating in this way, one will come closer and closer to the inherent clarity of the essence of mind.

Śamatha meditation, the meditation which brings this calmness and peace of mind, is done either "with a support" or "without a support." "With a support" means meditating on something like a Buddha statue, on the breath, or a visualization. This is an easier way to meditate, but one gradually needs to develop concentration that has no support. Śamatha "without a support" means settling the mind without settling on something. Usually, the way that we do this is to do śamatha meditation which is mainly focused on the freshness of whatever is happening in the present moment.

Analytical and Placement Meditation

Generally speaking there are two main approaches to meditation. First there is the "analytical meditation" of the great scholars, the great *paṇḍitas*. With this meditation one is very aware and investigates everything that is there. One examines the various objects to find out their substance, to find out if they exist, if they don't exist, to look at the nature of the external world, to look at the mind, and so on. One examines everything very minutely and carefully using meditation as a means of seeing things more and more sharply and precisely. Through this meditation a great deal of mental clarity and sharpness emerges, but not the calm abiding of the mind. So the first main approach is called the "analytical meditation of the great paṇḍitas."

The other main approach is called the actual abiding or placement meditation of the yogi. The word in Sanskrit is *kusulu* and this means "those who don't contrive or fabricate anything" or "those who are very simple and natural." One would call them "yogis" these days. In this meditation one doesn't analyze everything that is taking place. One learns instead how to bring the mind to rest, how to rest within the mind's very essence, and then how to develop the actual power of meditation through direct experience. One does not get caught up with thoughts of the past or future and learns to be in the freshness of the very instant. One then learns to actually lengthen this meditation so that one can rest moment after moment in the freshness. Through the actual experience of this one learns instinctively what is to be done in meditation and what is to be avoided.

To develop meditation one needs to actually meditate. To gain a genuine experience of meditation one first goes to a place which is favorable for meditation; a nice, calm, and isolated place. One then does many short sessions by meditating very clearly for a short while. One doesn't think of the past or future, but tries to experience that freshness of the present doing this again and again and again with many short clear sessions. Gradually one extends the time of each session so that one can have that freshness and sharpness of meditation for longer and longer periods.

The great meditators of the past have employed several different terms for this fresh state of meditation. They have used different terms which seem to be meaningful to them. One term is to meditate in that "freshness." This gives the idea of not being caught up in the past or future but being in the instant, fresh in the next instant, fresh in the instant after. Another term which means the same thing is the "natural awareness" of meditation. The word "natural" means unfabricated. This means that whatever is happening in that instant, one need not think about it or play with it. All mental analyzes are "unnatural" in that they are fabrications which occur when one thinks a lot about what is going on and tries to change it. This word "natural" is the opposite of "fabrication." Freshness and natural awareness apply more to the relaxation of meditation. If one has a sheaf of wheat and binds it with a rope, then it is bound very tightly. If one cuts the rope, then the wheat falls down loosely and naturally. So there is another term "loose" in meditation, but this word "loose" means more in Tibetan than in English. The idea of "loose" is the idea of taking away the tension and letting something be relaxed in the natural way rather than holding it together artificially. The Tibetan word for "freshness" is *song ga*. The Tibetan word for "natural awareness" is *nyu ma* or *nyu med shi pa*. The Tibetan word for "looseness" is *lu pa*. Then there is a fourth term which is *rig ki* which in Tibetan means something like "sharp." "Sharpness" is used in relation to meditation because there is this very attentive sharpness that one applies to mindfulness and awareness. In summary, these four terms are very powerful and have been applied by the great masters to meditation. As one meditates, one will encounter these four things and the impact of the meaning of these words then strikes home.

Insight Meditation

Previously, we mentioned that Buddhism and Hinduism have similar names for different things. The Buddhists talk of vipaśyanā or insight meditation. The Hindus also use this term because both religions had their roots in India and used the Sanskrit language. Even though the terms are the same for Buddhists and Hindus, vipaśyanā meditation in the Buddhist tradition is different from the vipaśyanā meditation of the Hindu tradition. In fact, there are also some different ways of defining vipaśyanā meditation within the different schools of Buddhism.

In the hīnayāna tradition of Buddhism there are two main stages of meditation: śamatha and vipaśyanā. But this is not quite the same thing as śamatha and vipaśyanā in the vajrayāna. Śamatha in the hīnayāna tradition is also different from śamatha in the vajrayāna tradition. To define these terms more accurately, when śamatha was translated into Tibetan it became *she nay*. The first syllable *she* means "calm" and syllable *nay* means "stability." So the first syllable is "calmness" and this means that one establishes a state of mind which is not troubled by many thoughts. By getting rid of all the problems associated with thoughts, a natural peace and calmness comes to the mind. Then, when that peace or absence of thoughts is there, the mind becomes very stable. So to translate *shinay* meditation literally would be "calm stability meditation." Vipaśyanā when it was translated into Tibetan became *lhag tong*. *Tong* means "to see" and means to have insight. From the sūtra point of view this means that one gains insight into the dharmatā or the universal essence. In the vajrayāna context it is translated in terms of "seeing the very essence of mind," or seeing the very nature of mind. So there is the insight, but this insight gains something which is *tong*. The *lhag* means "superior" because when one has insight, there is no more confusion of "Is it like this? Is it like that? Is its nature such and such?" One sees directly beyond any shadow of doubt so it literally means "superlative seeing."

One is trying to gain vipaśyanā insight into the very essence of things in both the sūtrayāna and the vajrayāna approach. In the sūtrayāna approach one is trying to gain insight into the essence of phenomena, the universal essence. In the vajrayāna approach one is trying to gain insight into the very essence of the mind. They are the same in nature because in both cases one is trying to penetrate to the very heart of phenomena, the very essence of what is there. If one discovers the nature of phenomena, then one discovers the nature of the mind as well. So śamatha and vipaśyanā are the same in their nature and purpose.

Where śamatha and vipaśyanā differ is in the means they employ to reach the goal. In the sūtrayāna one tackles all the various phenomena and tries to penetrate their essence by meditation. In the vajrayāna one knows it would be a difficult and lengthy task to work through the essence of all external phenomena as well as the internal phenomena of the mind. Instead if one discovers the universal essence in one thing completely, then it will realize the essence of everything else. It is therefore more convenient to meditate on one's own mind and discover the very essence of this mind. Discovering the essence of mind will automatically reveal the very essence of everything else in the external world. So this method is more rapid and focused. In this regard Gampopa says:

The view is the view of the mind itself.
If one looks and asks, "Where is the mind?"
One is never going to discover it.

Gampopa compared this to a traditional story of a man called Jig. This man was very strong physically but not too intelligent. He was unusual because he had a jewel in his forehead and rather floppy skin on his head. One day, when he was tired, the loose skin on his forehead flopped forward and covered up this jewel. In his tiredness and not being too bright, he thought, "Oh, it is gone!" He became very worried and started looking for it everywhere and just couldn't find it. He was very distressed and, of course, all the time it was in his forehead. It is like that: If we want to find the essence, then we turn to our own mind. That's where it is. If we look anywhere else and try to approach the essence through anything other than our mind, it will be very hard to discover.

Seeing Mind Directly

Usually a way of analyzing what one does is based on the view that one has, the meditation one does, and the practice that goes with this view. As far as the view is concerned, the sūtra approach and the vajrayāna approach are a bit different. The sūtra approach is called "the analytical approach" or "the approach of analyzing the mind." Through analysis and inspection one comes to the conclusion that mind's essence is empty, its quality is clarity, and that buddha essence exists in all beings. But this is derived mainly through the process of deduction.

The vajrayāna view is based on the mind itself. Rather than being deductive it is called "the direct experience." So one has the immediate experience of the mind. One discovers the mind as it is. Because of that immediate and real experience, the view of how the mind is will naturally arise. One begins by doing śamatha meditation. This calm stability of śamatha helps one gain the very direct experience of the mind. One looks at the arising, the abiding, and the departing of the things which take place in the mind.

First we examine arising. When something happens, a thought for instance, we try to discover where it comes from. It is different from the analytic approach because in the analytic approach if we have a happy thought, we then deduce that some pleasant object or action produced this happy thought. We would see a causal relationship of thought and object. In the vajrayāna, however, we are looking at the thought itself, looking for where has that thought actually come from? We try to see very clearly what source it emerged from. Second, we examine the actual thought the instant it is there; we try to find out where it actually is; where it is dwelling. And third, as the thought fades, we try to see very clearly where that thought has gone? Where has it departed to? By being aware of the arising, the abiding, and the departure of thoughts, we begin to see that there is no place, no thought bank that thoughts emerge from. There is also no actual place where they are located nor where we can find them. Finally, we discover there is no place that they go to afterwards. So all we find is emptiness in these three moments of thought.

By the repeated examination of thoughts, we gain stability of mind and begin to understand the essence of this mind itself. Once we become familiar with the nature of mind, we see that it is the same whether we are thinking or not thinking. We discover that the essence of the mind itself is very stable. Through this direct approach, we don't need other techniques to bring stability to the mind because, by discovering the nature of the mind, there will quite naturally be a stability, a calm, and peace. We discover that even the very essence of thoughts is peace. We don't need to eliminate or suppress thoughts. Instead we gain the actual experience without philosophizing about emptiness. We don't need to know that everything is emptiness, because emptiness is the nature of mind. The very nature of what is happening in our experience is emptiness without any need to think, "Is it?" or "Isn't it?" or having to put any labels onto it. It is obviously empty because it is actually there. The same is true with the clarity; we don't need to analyze clarity or think, "Is this the clarity and the wisdom aspect?" because we arrive at a state where everything is apparent.

We no longer need to add any terms or ideas or philosophy since the actual experience is there.

For instance, before we began our meditation practice, our anger was very powerful and overtook us and seemed very strong and important. Then we learned to look at our mind and to look at how we got angry and where the anger came from. Then we looked at the anger which seemed so real to find its essence. We saw there was nothing there to be found when looking at it straight on.

When we meditate, we sometimes develop a very stable and calm state and think, "Oh yes, my meditation is really working." Sometimes we have many thoughts and think, "Now there are too many thoughts." But when we look at the stable mind and the busy, thinking mind, we do not find a difference between these states from the essence of mind. This contrasts with our normal conception of mind. Sometimes we think, "Now I'm in meditation" and another time we think, "Now I'm thinking" and still another time "Now I'm happy" or "Now I'm sad" or "Now I'm getting angry and upset." It seems there is a tremendous amount of change in the mind, but when we learn to be aware of the nature of the mind, we find this nature is identical in all these reflections.

To improve our meditation and make it a continuous living experience, we need faith and devotion. It is said in the Kagyu lineage prayer that: "Devotion is the head of meditation." We pray to open ourself, to have confidence in our guru, in the gurus of the transmission, and all the buddhas, the bodhisattvas, and yidams. It is by making this connection with them, with full devotion towards them, and having that confidence in them, that produces this deep meditation. Once our meditation is more and more stable, things become clearer and clearer and all the various good qualities emerge. That is why we do the various sādhanas and devotional practices.

When meditation progresses and becomes part of us, we can find peace. Then when thoughts of aggression and aversion begin to arise, we find peace by meditating on their essence. When thoughts of desire or attraction emerge, then by being aware of the essence of these thoughts we find peace. When feelings of suffering start to emerge, we are able to go to their essence and experience calm and peace. When thoughts of happiness that stimulate pride and artificial joy emerge, by going to the essence, we again find peace. Through this very deep awareness of the essence of everything peacefulness permeates.

The Main Obstacles to Meditation

The two main obstacles to meditation are sluggishness and excitement. Sluggishness is when our meditation becomes very heavy, very unclear, very thick, and full of torpor. This drowsiness feels heavy and there is a lack of clarity. That's the first obstacle to meditation. The second obstacle is excitement when our mind is overstimulated. We have many thoughts of the past or the current of thoughts are so strong that our mind just can't be settled.

In more detail, there are six difficulties or obstacles to meditation. First is too much wanting, too much desire. This occurs when we are thinking, "Oh, I want to be happy, I must be happy. I want to go and amuse myself and go and see this or that particular event." Or we feel we ought to be a certain way or we feel a great pull towards something. By itself this is not always an obstacle to meditation. But when it becomes so strong that our mind keeps going back to that thing over and over it is detrimental for meditation. For example, we may think "I want a nice house" and then think of what the house is going to look like, how it is going to be built, and so on.

The second obstacle is having an aggressive mind. This occurs when we think about hurting other people, how we want to fight back with someone who has harmed us. We want to say something that will really put them in their place. These thoughts aren't necessarily an obstacle but when they become so dominant and the mind is so drawn into them we aren't achieving stability in meditation, then this becomes a fault.

Obviously, these obstacles are things we need to eliminate in ourselves. This is why we do the Kagyu Lineage prayer at the beginning of each meditation session. The prayer says "weariness of saṃsāra is the foot of meditation." The actual word in Tibetan for "weariness" is *shen lok* which means "to turn one's back on craving" or "to turn away from wanting and craving." We need a strong foundation for our meditation, this we need to turn away from the powerful pull of desire which dominates our mind.

Some people when they encounter the expression *shen lok* (it usually has the feeling of disgust with saṃsāra) think that to be a Buddhist one has to wear torn clothes, eat the simplest food, live in a rundown house, and choose an impoverished country to live in. To be a Buddhist doesn't mean that one wears rags, eats terrible food, and so on. It means that one doesn't have powerful desires that leads to "I really must have that thing. I can't live without it. I deserve this and living without it isn't right." It means one doesn't think, "This is too important to me. I can't give it away because it means too much to me." When desire is that strong, it presents an obstacle to one's practice. *Shen lok* or "disgust with saṃsāra" literally means "turning away from desire." It means detaching oneself from those desires, involvements which represent obstacles because one can't let go. Buddha himself said:

If one doesn't have desire, then it is perfectly all right
　　to own a house of a thousand stories.
If one has desire, then one needs to give up attachment
　　to even a miserable mud hut.
If one doesn't have desire, then it is all right to possess a
　　thousand measures of gold.

If one has desire, then one needs to give up one's attachment to even a worthless object.

So, the main point is not attachment to the objects themselves, but one's attitude towards these objects.

The third obstacle to meditation is mental obscurity which occurs when our mind is not clear, when it is heavy and thick. The fourth obstacle to meditation occurs when that obscurity becomes sleep. We are so sluggish that we fall asleep. The fifth obstacle is excitement or overstimulation which occurs when we are too excited by the power of thoughts. The sixth obstacle is regret which occurs when we feel sorry about something that has happened and keep going back to it during meditation.

From time to time one of these obstacles comes up in our practice. When they pop up, we must first of all recognize them for what they are and then decide not to be swayed from doing meditation by them because meditation will allow us to go beyond them. For instance, if we have this sadness or regret for something in the past, then we recognize it in our meditation and think, "Oh yes, today I'm being overwhelmed by regret. I must go beyond regret through meditation." We use meditation to help get rid of this unnecessary regret. If we are aggressive, we must think, "Yes, today I have a lot of aggression. I must meditate in order to get over that aggression by using meditation to help annihilate aggression." If we feel the great attraction of desire and involvement with a project, then we think, "Today I will meditate to remove that particular obstacle." Approaching it this way will allow us to work with it and diminish its power over our meditation.

These are the six main obstacles of meditation. The most important ones are sluggishness and excitement. In order to cope with these two main obstacles, we can employ visualization. When we are very sluggish, dull, thick and heavy, we can recall the qualities of the Buddha, the three jewels, the dharma, and the qualities of *samādhi* and meditation. This should perk us up a bit. We can also visualize a white drop of light in our heart moving up to the crown of the head and staying there for a while. This will help with sluggishness. When the problem is excitement, we need to tone down the mind a little. We remember all of the drawbacks of saṃsāra, all the suffering it involves, and all of the problems caused by the defilements. We can also visualize a black drop in our heart that slowly sinks down into the seat on which we are sitting. It is said that those two techniques will help with the problems of sluggishness and excitement.

When we start meditation, it is important to do many short sessions rather than a few long sessions of meditation. So we try to meditate very sharply for a short while and then stop. Then we have a break and do another meditation session. Each time is short, sharp, and clear and it feels like a pleasant experience. If one tries to meditate too long, it becomes exhausting and the association of tiredness with meditation is not going to help. That's one of the reasons for doing short sessions at first. Also, thinking of meditation as a pleasant experience makes us very keen to do it again. If we see the benefits of sitting just for a little while and having this moment of clarity and precision, then we appreciate it and want to do it again and again to perfect it. Once we are used to it, we should start increasing the length of the sessions slowly so that we increase the amount of clarity. When we have the taste of meditation and begin to understand what meditation is, we need to increase and develop that meditation. We need to develop it constantly going from one degree of stability to an even greater degree of stability. Three things which help us do this are called "integrating defilements into the path," "integrating happiness and sadness into the path," and "integrating sickness into the path."

"Integrating the defilements into the path" is turning desires, aggression, stupidity, pride, jealousy and so on into good qualities.

Of these aggression or anger is by far the most powerful defilement. We think the situation is so unbearable that we feel we have to explode, hit someone, shout at somebody. If we are under the influence of anger, we try to look at it directly and find out where it is at the time the actual anger arises. "Where is the anger coming from? Where is it welling up from? Where is this actual instant?" and "Where does it go?" If we face it directly, it cannot actually be grasped. We feel angry, but when we look for it, we cannot find out where it resides. If we try to stay within this realm of nonexistence, this realm of not meeting the anger itself, the anger should be reduced a little bit. By learning to stay within this nonexistence of the arising, abiding, and departing of the anger, then gradually over a period of time we will really eliminate the influence of anger from our life.

This same approach works not only with aggression, but also with desire, pride, jealousy—all of the defilements. Each time we look for the defilement, we find only emptiness and experience this emptiness through direct experience discovering its essence. In the sūtra approach, we develop an understanding of emptiness mainly through a process of deduction and investigation based on logic, clues, and reasonings. We eventually come to the conclusion of the emptiness of emotions based on the investigation of such facts as what we did when we examined the long and short sticks. Through these kinds of exercises the nature of emptiness is developed in the sūtra approach.

The vajrayāna approach is much more vivid, immediate, and real. When anger arises, for instance, the anger is truly there. It is very strong and potent at the time. Rather than analyzing and thinking about it, we look at it straight in the face and try to find out, "Where are you? Where are you coming from?" We look directly rather than using deductive reasoning. The result is the the emptiness of the anger is experienced. This way of tackling the emotions and defilements is often described in the *spiritual songs*

(Skt. *dohās*) of the siddhas. They tell how powerful and vivid anger can be and how, at the same time, we can use anger to discover the emptiness of phenomena because we naturally meet emptiness when we look directly at this powerful and vivid emotion.

These two approaches of direct experience of the vajrayāna and the inferential approach of the sūtra path is described by the Third Karmapa, Rangjung Dorje, in *The Aspirational Prayer of Mahāmudrā* :[19]

The way things really are cannot be phrased in terms of existence.

So he says the defilements or even the mind itself do not exist. When one seeks them, one can never encounter their existence. And then he says:

*Not even the Buddhas can see
    the true existence of any of these things.*

So it is not a question of existence or of nonexistence because even the Buddhas cannot see its existence. On the other hand, one can't talk about total annihilation or nonexistence either because out of this is reflected saṃsāra (the impure side) and nirvāṇa (which is liberation). Whether one is in saṃsāra or whether one is in nirvāṇa depends on one's mind and so the next line of this prayer says:

*It is not nonexistence because therein lies
    the foundation of saṃsāra and nirvāṇa.*

One might think that if things are not existent and not nonexistent, there is some kind of contradiction here. No, there isn't, because things manifest in the middle way, which is the union of saṃsāra and nirvāṇa. It is neither one extreme of existence, nor the other extreme of total annihilation. So it continues:

It is not contradictory.
   It is this fusion, which is the Middle-way.

And the last line of the prayer is:

May that which is free from any extremes
   —the universal essence, the essence of everything—be realized.

Freedom from extremes means to be free from the *four extremes* and the *eight intellectual complications.* It's a little strange when one starts talking in terms of nonexistence and not nonexistence because this is not easy to grasp intellectually. But, as far as the actual practice is concerned, when one meditates, these words develop full meaning because one discovers the essence of things and the truth and meaning of those words becomes lucid. To develop peace and insight then is really just seeing phenomena as they really are. Sometimes when one meditates, it goes really well and one thinks, "Oh, now I've really got it. At last I'm a really good meditator, a great practitioner." Sometimes it goes really poorly and one thinks, "Oh, there's no hope. I've lost the knack of meditating completely." Both are just attitudes of the mind. Whether one feels one has great or terrible meditation, it doesn't make a difference to the actual essence, which always remains the same. One just continues to meditate without being carried away by the "goodness" or the "badness" of the experience. One just continues meditation no matter how we may relate to the experience.

Notes

1. The technical terms are italicized the first time to indicate that they are defined in the Glossary of Terms.
2. In the Buddhist view the ordinary reality that we see is actually a delusion. This is called relative reality. Only with great spiritual attainment can we see through this delusion and perceive absolute reality and see "things as they really are" (Tib. *nga lu*).
3. The Tibetan words are given as they are pronounced, not as they are spelled. For the Tibetan spelling see the Glossary of Tibetan Terms.
4. There is "gom" (spelled *sgom*) which means "meditation" and "khom" (spelled *goms*) which means "to habituate." These words are very close having the same root.
5. During this talk Thrangu Rinpoche was pointing to a brass pot in front of him.
6. Buddhists believe in what has been incorrectly called "the transmigration of the soul." Rather in reincarnation the karmic aspect of mind passes on from one lifetime to the next.
7. For the last sixteen lifetimes, the Karmapa has written a letter before his death stating where and when he would be reborn and giving his name and his parent's name. This letter is opened years after his death and has always been accurate.
8. For a detailed description of the vinaya see Thrangu Rinpoche's *Teachings on the Tibetan Vinaya*. Namo Buddha Publications.
9. Buddhist monks follow about 125 vows and Buddhist nuns follow about 320 vows.
10. In Buddhism, the deliberate killing of any animal will lead to negative karma.

11. These are the teachings of śūnyatā (Sanskrit) which has been translated as "emptiness" because the essential nature of everything is "empty." But this emptiness is not like empty space because all phenomena comes out of or manifests from this emptiness. Therefore we prefer "emptiness" to "voidness" which we reserve for completely empty as in "empty space."
12. For a detailed account of Buddha-nature see Thrangu Rinpoche's *The Uttara Tantra: A Treatise on Buddha-nature.* Namo Buddha Publications.
13. These are transcendent generosity, conduct, patience, diligence, and knowledge (Skt. *prajñā*) plus skillful means, aspirational prayers, the powers, and wisdom (Skt. *yeshe*).
14. These "channels" refer to the subtle or psychic channels (Skt. *nādī*, Tib. *tsa*), not anatomical ones which are much like the meridians in acupuncture, in which energies, or "winds" (Skt. *prāṇa*, Tib. *lung*) travel.
15. There are three levels of practice. The outer is external activities such as making offerings, the inner is making a mental commitment, and the secret involves changing the energies of the body.
16. Thrangu Rinpoche belongs to the Kagyu lineage and so he uses these lineage holders. Members of different sects would, of course, visualize a different set of lineage holders.
17. These are extensively described in Thrangu Rinpoche's *The Four Ordinary Foundations of Buddhist Practice.* Namo Buddha Publications.
18. This is primarily the practice of mahāmudrā in the Kagyu or dzogchen in the Nyingma tradition. See Thrangu Rinpoche's *The Moonlight of Mahāmudā: The Direct Meditation on Mind.* Snow Lion Publications.
19. For a translation and commentary on this spiritual song see Thrangu Rinpoche's *The Aspiration Prayer for Mahāmudā* Namo Buddha Publications.

The Glossary of Terms

Those not familiar with pronouncing Sanskrit can use the following five rules.
The ś and the ṣ are pronounced "sh" so śamatha is pronounced "shamatha" and vipaśyanā is pronounced "vipashyana."
The c is always pronounced "ch" so bodhicitta is pronounced "bodhichita."
The ṛ is pronounced "ri" so that amṛta is pronounced "amrita."
The ā and ī are pronounced as short vowels so hīnayāna is pronounced "hinayana," but the ū is pronounced as a long u so sūtra is pronounced "sootra."
The consonants with diacritic marks are pronounced as they sound so saṅgha is pronounced "sangha" and ḍāka is pronounced "daka."

Abhidharma (Tib. *chö ngön pa*) The Buddhist teachings are often divided into the Tripiṭaka: the sūtras (teachings of the Buddha), the Vinaya (teachings on conduct), and the Abhidharma which are the analyzes of phenomena that exist primarily as a commentarial tradition to the Buddhist teachings.

absolute truth (Tib. *dondam*) There are two truths or views of reality—relative truth which is seeing things as ordinary beings do with the dualism of "I" and "other" and absolute truth, also called ultimate truth, which is transcending duality and seeing things as they are.

amṛta (Tib. *dut tsi*) A blessed substance which can cause spiritual and physical healing.

ātman Sanskrit for a permanent "self" which exists after death.

bodhicitta (Tib. *chang chup chi sem*) Literally, the mind of enlightenment. There are two kinds of bodhicitta: absolute bodhicitta which is completely awakened mind that sees the emptiness of phenomena and relative bodhicitta which is the aspiration to practice the six pāramitās and to free all beings from the sufferings of samsāra.

bodhisattva (Tib. *chang chup sem pa*) An individual who has committed him or herself to the mahāyāna path of compassion and the practice of the six pāramitās to achieve Buddhahood to free all beings from saṃsāra.

Buddha-nature (Skt. *tathāgatagarbha*, Tib. *deshin shekpai nying po*) The original nature present in all beings which when realized leads to enlightenment. It is often called the essence of Buddhahood or enlightened essence.

completion stage (Tib. *dzo rim*) In the vajrayāna there are two stages of meditation: the creation and the completion stage. The completion stage is a method of tantric meditation in which one attains bliss, clarity, and nonthought by means of the subtle channels and energies within the body.

creation stage (Tib. *che rim*) In the vajrayāna there are two stages of meditation: the creation and the completion stage. In this stage the visualization of the deity is built up and maintained.

ḍāka (Tib. *da po*) A male counterpart to a ḍākinī.

ḍākinī (Tib. *khandro*) A yoginī who has attained high realizations of the fully enlightened mind. She may be a human being who has achieved such attainments or a non-human manifestation of the enlightened mind of a meditational deity.

dharma (Tib. *chö*) This has two main meanings: Any truth such as the sky is blue and secondly, as it is used in this text, the teachings of the Buddha.

dharmacakra (Skt. for "wheel of dharma") The Buddha's teachings correspond to three levels: the hīnayāna, the mahāyāna and the vajrayāna with each level being one turning of the wheel of dharma.

dharmatā (Tib. *chö nyi*) The true nature of phenomena, not phenomena as it appears to us, and is often translated as "suchness" or "the true nature of things," or "things as-they-are."

dharmadhātu (Tib. *chö ying*) The all-encompassing space which is unoriginated and beginningless out of which all phenomena arise.

dohā (Tib. *gur*) A spiritual song spontaneously composed by a vajrayāna practitioner. It usually has nine syllables per line.

eight intellectual complications Something without the eight mental fabrications is (1) without a beginning, (2) without a cessation, (3) without nihilism, (4) without eternalism, (5) without going, (6) without coming, (7) not being separate, and (8) not being non-separate.

five paths (Tib. *lam nga*) Traditionally, a practitioner goes through five stages or paths to enlightenment. These are (1) The path of accumulation which emphasizes purifying one's obscurations and accumulating merit. (2) The path of junction or application in which the meditator develops profound understanding of the four noble truths and cuts the root to the desire realm. (3) The path of insight or seeing in which the meditator develops greater insight and enters the first bodhisattva level. (4) The path of meditation in which the meditator cultivates insight in the second through tenth bodhisattva levels. (5) The path of fulfillment which is the complete attainment of Buddhahood.

four extremes (Skt. *catuṣkoṭi*, Tib. *mu shi*) These are a belief in the existence of everything (also called "eternalism"), a belief that nothing exists (also called "nihilism"), a belief that things exist and don't exist, and that reality is something other than existence and non-existence.

four foundations of meditation (Tib. *tun mong gi ngon dro shi*) These are the four thoughts that turn the mind. They are reflection on precious human birth, impermanence and the inevitability of death, karma and its effects, and the pervasiveness of suffering in saṃsāra.

four immeasurables (Tib. *tsad med pa*) These are limitless love, limitless compassion, limitless joy, and limitless impartiality.

four noble truths (Tib. *pak pay den pa shi*) The Buddha began teaching with a talk in India at Sarnath on the four noble truths. These are the truth of suffering, the truth of the cause of suffering, the cessation of suffering, and the eight-fold path. These truths are the foundation of Buddhism, particularly the Theravāda path.

four special foundations (Tib. *ngöndro*, pronounced "nun dro") These are the four ngöndro practices of taking refuge with prostrations, vajrasattva mantra, maṇḍala offering, and guru yoga practice. For ngöndro one does approximately 100,000 prostrations, 100,000 vajrasattva mantras, 100,000 maṇḍala offerings, and 100,000 guru yogas.

guru yoga The fourth practice of the preliminary practices of ngögdro which emphasizes devotion to one's guru.

healing nectar (Skt. *amṛita*, Tib. *dut tsi*) A blessed substance which can cause spiritual and physical healing.

hīnayāna (Tib. *tek pa chung wa*) Literally, the lesser vehicle. The term refers to the first teachings of the Buddha which emphasized the careful examination of mind and its confusion. Also called the Theravāda path.

interdependent origination (Tib. *ten drel*) The theory that all phenomena are interdependent. There are twelve links to this origination called the nidānas.

jñāna (Tib. *ye she*) Literally "primordial awareness." This is the wisdom that manifests at enlightenment when the mind is no longer obscured.

karma (Tib. *lay*) Literally "action." Karma is a universal law that when one does a wholesome action, one's circumstances will improve and when one does an unwholesome action, negative results will eventually occur from the act.

kāyas, three (Tib. *ku sum*) There are three bodies of the Buddha: the nirmāṇakāya, sambhogakāya, and dharmakāya. The dharmakāya, also called the "truth body," is the complete enlightenment or the complete wisdom of the Buddha which is unoriginated wisdom beyond form and manifests in the sambhogakāya and the nirmāṇakāya. The sambhogakāya, also called the "enjoyment body," manifests only to bodhisattvas. The nirmāṇakāya, also called the "emanation body," and manifests in the world and in this context manifests as the Śākyamuni Buddha.

kleśa *(Tib. nyon mong pa)* Disturbing emotions and is usually translated as "defilement" in this text. The three main disturbing emotions are (passion or desire or attachment), (aggression or anger) and (ignorance or delusion or aversion.) The five poisons are the three above plus pride and jealousy.

kusulu There are two approaches; one is to study the Buddhist texts and the other is to meditate directly with little study and this is the kusulu way.

mahāyāna (Tib. *tek pa chen po*) Literally, the "great vehicle." These are the teachings of the second turning of the wheel of dharma which emphasizes emptiness.

mahāpaṇḍita (Tib. *paṇ ḍi ta chen po*) A great Buddhist scholar (paṇḍita).

maṇḍala (Tib. *chin kor*) A diagram used in vajrayāna practices which usually has a central deity and four directions.

mantra (Tib. *ngak*) Sanskrit syllables which represent various energies which are repeated in different vajrayāna.

Middle-way (Tib. *u ma*) or Madhyamaka School. A philosophical school founded by Nāgārjuna and is based on the Prāṇapāramitā sūtras of emptiness.

nirvāṇa (Tib. *nya ngen lay day pa*) A state of no more suffering achieved when one is completely enlightened. Used in contrast to saṃsāra.

nirmāṇakāya See kāyas, three.

phowa (Tib.) An advanced tantric practice concerned with the ejection of consciousness at death to a favorable realm.

paṇḍita (Tib. *paṇ ḍi ta*) A great scholar.

prajñā (Tib. *sherab*) Sanskrit for "perfect knowledge" and can mean wisdom, understanding, or discrimination. Usually it means the wisdom of seeing things from a high (e.g. nondualistic) point of view.

pāramitā (Tib. *pha rol tu phyin pa*) Sanskrit for "transcendent perfections." These are the six practices of the mahāyāna path: Transcendent generosity, transcendent discipline, transcendent patience, transcendent exertion, transcendent meditation, and transcendent knowledge (prajñā) plus skillful means, power, and enlightened wisdom (skt. jñāna).

rinpoche Literally, "very precious" and is used as a term of respect for a Tibetan guru.

relative truth (Tib. *kunsop*) There are two truths: relative and absolute truth. Relative truth is the perception of an ordinary (unenlightened) person who sees the world with all his or her projections based on the false belief in ego.

sādhana (Tib. *drup top*) A tantric ritual text which details how to attain meditative realization of a specific maṇḍala of deities.

Śākya Paṇḍita A hereditary head of the Śākya lineage. A great scholar (1181-1251 C.E.) who was an outspoken opponent of the Kagyu teachings. He also became head of the Tibetan state under the authority of the Mongol emperors.

samādhi (Tib. *ting nge dzin*) Also called "meditative absorption" or "one-pointed meditation" and is the highest form of meditation in which the mind remains in meditation without any distraction.

śamatha or tranquillity meditation (Tib. *she nay*). This is basic sitting meditation. The aim of śamatha meditation is to be able to place the mind on an object and remain there without distraction.

saṃsāra (Tib. *kor wa*) Conditioned existence which is ordinary suffering in life which occurs because one still possesses passion, aggression, and ignorance. It is contrasted to nirvāṇa.

saṅgha (Tib. *gen dun*) Companions on the path. They may be the regular saṅgha who are all the persons on the path or the noble saṅgha who are the realized ones.

siddha (Tib. *grub thob*) An accomplished Buddhist practitioner.
siddhi (Tib. *ngö drub*) Spiritual accomplishments of accomplished practitioners.
skandha (Tib. *pang pa*) Literally "heaps" and are the five basic transformations that perceptions undergo when an object is perceived. These are form, feeling, perception, formation, and consciousness.
spiritual song (Skt. *dohā*, Tib. *gur*) A religious song spontaneously composed by a vajrayāna practitioner. It usually has nine syllables per line.
subtle channels (Skt. *nāḍī*, Tib. *tsa*) These "channels" refer to the subtle channels which are not anatomical ones, but pathways that subtle energies or "winds" (Skt. *prāṇa*, Tib. *lung*) travel.
śūnyatā (Skt., Tib. *tong pa nyi*) Translated as "voidness" or "emptiness." The Buddha taught in the second turning of the wheel of dharma that external phenomena and the self or "I" have no inherent existence and therefore are "empty."
sūtra (Tib. *do*) The hīnayāna and mahāyāna texts which are the words of the Buddha. These are often contrasted with the tantras which are the vajrayāna teachings and the śāstras which are commentaries on the words of the Buddha.
sūtrayāna The sūtra approach to achieving enlightenment which includes the hīnayāna and the mahāyāna. In this book this refers to studying and analyzing the teachings of the Buddha rather than the mahāmudrā approach.
tantra (Tib. *gyu*) The teachings of the vajrayāna.
three immutables These are the hīnayāna, the mahāyāna, and the vajrayāna.
three jewels (Tib. *kön chok sum*) These are the Buddha, the dharma (the teachings of the Buddha), and the saṅgha (the companions on the path).
Theravāda (Skt. *sthaviravādin*, Tib. *neten depa*) One of the four main orders of the hīnayāna school in India. This tradition has

been maintained in Thailand, Burma, Cambodia, and Sri Lanka.
Theravādin A follower of the Theravāda school.
three roots (Tib. *tsa wa sum*) These are the lamas, the yidams, and the dharma protectors.
Tirthikas Religious people who believe in a personal self.
tranquillity meditation See śamatha meditation.
two truths See relative and absolute truth.
vajra (Tib. *dorje*) This is either an implement used in vajrayāna practice or it denotes something which is indestructible such as in "vajra nature."
vajrayāna (Tib. *dorje tek pa*) There are three major types of Buddhist practices. The hīnayāna, the mahāyāna and the vajrayāna which emphasizes the clarity aspect of phenomena and is mainly practiced in Tibet.
vinaya (Tib. *dul wa*) These are the teachings by the Buddha concerning proper conduct. There are seven main precepts that may be observed by lay persons or 125 or 320 to be observed by monks and nuns.
vipaśyāna meditation Sanskrit for "insight meditation" (Tib. *lhag tong*) This meditation as used in this book refers to meditation into the fundamental nature of phenomena. It is closely related to śamatha meditation in that one needs the calm, one-pointed concentration of śamatha meditation to accomplish this.
wheel of dharma (Skt. *dharmacakra*) The Buddha's teachings correspond to three levels: the hīnayāna, the mahāyāna and the vajrayāna with each set being one turning.
yāna (Tib. *thek pa*) Literally, "vehicle" but refers here to level of teaching. There are three main yānas (the hīnayāna, mahāyāna, and vajrayāna).
yidam A vajrayāna practitioner's personal deity.
yogi (Tib. *nal yor*) An accomplished practitioner who usually chooses an unconventional lifestyle.

Glossary of Tibetan Terms

Pronounced	Transliterated	English
chang chup chi sem	byang chup kyi sems	bodhicitta
chang chup sem pa	byang chub sems dpa	bodhisattva
che rim	bskyed rim	creation stage
cho	chos	dharma
cho ngon pa	chos mngon pa	Abhidharma
cho ying	chos dbyings	dharmadhātu
chag pa	chags pa	desire
ngö drub	dngos grub	siddhis
do	mdo	sūtra
dondam	don dam pa'i bden pa	absolute truth
dorje	rdo rje	vajra
dorje teg pa	rdo rje theg pa	varjayāna
dpa po	dpa' bo	dāka
dul wa	'dul ba	Vinaya
dutsi	bdud rtsi	healing nectar
dzo rim	rdzogs rim	completion stage
gen dun	dge 'dun	saṅgha
genyan	dge bsnyen	lay precepts
gom	sgom	meditation
gom lam	sgom lam	path meditation
gur	mgur	spiritual song
gyu	rgyud	tantra
je gom	dpyad sgom	analytical med.
jin lop	byin rlaps	blessings
khandro	mkha' 'gro ma	ḍākinī
khom	goms	habituate
kön chok sum	dkon mchog gsum	three jewels
kor wa	'khor ba	saṃsāra

ku sum	sku gsum	three kāyas
kunsop	kun rdzob kyi bden pa	relative truth
lhag tong	lhag mthong	vipaśyanā
lay	las	karma
lung	rlung	subtle wind
mö pa	mos pa	aspiration
neten depa	gnas brtan pa' sde pa	Theravāda
ngak	sngags	mantra
ngö drub	grub thob	siddha
nya ngen lay day pa	mya ngan las 'das pa	nirvāṇa
nyon mong	nyon mongs	kleśa
pak pay den pa shi	'phags pa'i bden pa bzhi	four truths
pandita	paṇḍita	scholar
phowa	'pho ba	ejection practice
pung po	phung po	skanda
sang gay	sangs rgyas	the Buddha
sang gnak	gsangs snags	secret mantra
she nay	zhi gnas	śamatha
she wa	zhi ba	peace
sherab	shes rab	prajñā
ta ma pa	tsad mrd pa	4 immeasurables
teg pa	theg pa	vehicle
tek pa chen po	theg pa chen po	mahāyāna
tek pa cung wa	theg pa chung ba	hīnayāna
tendrel	rten 'brel	dependent origin.
tin ne dzin	ting nge 'dzin	samādhi
toma	gtor ma	cake offering
tsa	rtsa	subtle channels
tsa wa sum	rtsa ba gsum	three roots
tsultrim	tshul khrims	discipline
un ma	dbu ma	Madhyamaka
ye she	ye shes	wisdom (jñāna)

Bibliography

Asanga and Maitreya. *The Uttara Tantra*. *The Uttara Tantra* is one of the five books which Asanga received from the Maitreya Buddha. This book is a detailed description of Buddha-nature and is studied by all sects in Tibet as one of the foundations of the mahāyāna path. For a translation of the root text and a commentary by Thrangu Rinpoche see *The Uttara Tantra: A Treatise on Buddha-nature*. (Boulder, Colorado: Namo Buddha Publications).

Gampopa. *The Jewel Ornament of Liberation*. Gampopa one of the founders of the Kagyu lineage and wrote this book to explain basic dharma to his students. This book has been translated by Konchog Gyaltsen Rinpoche as *The Jewel Ornament of Liberation* (Ithaca, New York: Snow Lion Publications).

Thrangu Rinpoche. *Teachings on the Tibetan Vinaya.* (Boulder: Namo Buddha Publications.) This book describes the three vows (the hīnayāna, mahāyāna, and vajrayāna) involved in Buddhist conduct.

Thrangu Rinpoche. *The Four Ordinary Foundations of Buddhist Practice.* (Boulder: Namo Buddha Publications.) This book is a companion to the *Three Vehicles* and describes the four thoughts that one should contemplate before practicing.

Thrangu Rinpoche. *Moonbeams of Mahāmudrā: The Direct Meditation on Mind.* (Ithaca, New York: Snow Lion Publications.) A detailed overview of mahāmudrā meditation which is the principle meditation of the Kagyu lineage of Tibet.

Thrangu Rinpoche. *The Open Door to Emptiness.*(Boulder: Namo Buddha Publications.) A detailed explanation of Middle-way reasonings demonstrating emptiness.

Biographical Sketch of Thrangu Rinpoche

Khenpo Thrangu Rinpoche was born in Kham, Tibet in 1933. At the age of five he was formally recognized by the Sixteenth Karmapa and the Palpung Situ Rinpoche as the incarnation of the great Thrangu Tulku.

Entering Thrangu Monastery in Tibet, from the ages of six to seventeen he studied reading, writing, grammar, poetry, and astrology. He also memorized numerous texts and completed two preliminary retreats. At the age of sixteen under the guidance of Khenpo Lodro Rabsel, he began the extensive study of the three vehicles of Buddhism and spent more time in retreat. At the age of twenty-three along with Garwang and Chogyam Trungpa Rinpoche he received the Gelong ordination from the Gyalwa Karmapa. Following this Thrangu Rinpoche engaged in a period of intense practice and received further instructions from his lama Khenpo Gyangasha Wangpo.

When Rinpoche was twenty-seven years old, he narrowly escaped the Chinese troops in the invasion of Tibet and he and Khenpo Karthar were one of the few from his monastery to survive. With the loss of all the Buddhist texts from Tibet, he was called to Rumtek in Sikkim by His Holiness Karmapa and was given the task of reconstructing the teachings of the Kagyu lineage. He went to Buxador monastic refugee camp in Bengal and studied there under great scholars of all the Tibetan sects. At the age of thirty-five he was one of the first Kagyu lamas in recent history to obtain a geshe degree and received the highest degree of Geshe Lharampa from the Dalai Lama.

Returning to Rumtek Thrangu Rinpoche was appointed "Vice Chancellor of the Principal Seat of the Kagyu Vajra Upholder of the Three Disciplines" by His Holiness Karmapa and became the abbot of Nalanda Institute of Higher Learning. For the next twenty years he taught the tulkus of this monastic college including the four principal Kagyu tulkus: Shamar Rinpoche, Tai Situ Rinpoche, Jamgong Kongtrul Rinpoche, and Gyaltsab Rinpoche.

In 1976 Thrangu Rinpoche accompanied the Sixteenth Karmapa to Nepal and after that decided to build his own monastery just a few hundred feet from the Great Stupa in Boudhanath. Soon afterwards, Thrangu Rinpoche began teaching Western students in the Kathmandu area and purchased Namo Buddha, an extremely sacred site where one of the previous Buddhas had given his flesh to a tigress. His students also published Rinpoche's first book translated into English entitled *The Open Door to Emptiness*, an exposition of Madhyamaka logic.

In 1980 Thrangu Rinpoche was invited to Samye Ling monastery in Scotland and there he taught many of the same topics he had taught at Rumtek to Western students over the next three summers. He began with *The Uttara Tantra* and the *Jewel Ornament of Liberation* and supplemented these teachings with this teaching on the *Three Vehicles* to give a background on these topics.

For the last twenty years Thrangu Rinpoche has been traveling tirelessly in the West and to his centers in the Far East giving extensive teachings in over twenty countries on a whole range of topics. He is particularly known as a holder of the Shentong view and as a master of mahāmudrā meditation. He is recognized as having personal realization and is thus able to take complex Buddhist topics and make them accessible to Western students.

For more details on Thrangu Rinpoche's life, seminars, and publications please visit his website at: www.pe.net/~kml or contact Namo Buddha Publications at 1390 Kalmia Avenue, Boulder, CO 80304-1813, Phone: (303) 449-6608, Fax: (303) 440-0882. E-mail: cjohnson@ix.netcom.com

Index

Abhidharma 27
absolute level 12, 53-54
aggregates (skandha) 30, 33, 35-36
analytical meditation 92-93, 72
aspiration (möpa) 55
atman (permanent soul) 72
attachmen to saṃsāra 28, 55-56, 59, 100-101
beginningless time 30-32
belief in self 21
blessings 74-76, 88
bodhicitta 47, 49
bodhisattva 45-47, 48-50, 63-65, 81
Buddha, the 67, 74-75, 77
Buddha-nature 58-62, 67
compassion 45-49
conditioned existence (saṃsāra) 24, 28-29, 37-38, 100, 104
creation and completion stage 74, 78
ḍāka and ḍākinī 74
desire (chagpa) 55
diligence 64-65
discipline 39-40,
defilements (kleśa) 16-17, 22, 37, 59-60, 102-104
dharma protectors 81
dharmadhātu 57, 84
dharmatā 62
emptiness 29, 35, 50-51, 57-58, 78, 97, 104
five paths 23-28
four extremes 105
four immeasurables 46-50
four noble truths 13-23, 26-28, 37-38, 48
four ordinary foundations 83
four preliminary practices 82-83
Gampopa 95
genyan vows 40
guru, importance 74, 76-77, 87, 99
guru yoga 75-76
habituation (khom) 26, 65
healing nectar (amṛita) 49
insight meditation 73, 93-96
interdependent origination 33-34, 37, 50-54
jnañasattva 81
karma 16-17, 19-22, 26, 37, 71
Karmapa 34, 76, 104
Kagyu lineage Prayer 98
kleśa see defilements
luminosity (salwa) 57-58
mantras 63, 68, 73, 80-81
meditation 25-26, 28-38, 46, 65-66, 72-73, 78-80, 88-106
meditation directly on mind 78-80, 83-85, 87-91, 96-99
meditation obstacles 99-104
meditation posture 85-87
nirvāṇa 28, 104

nirvāṇa 28, 104
paṇḍita 92
pāramitās 56, 62-66, 73
paths, five 23-28
Patrul Rinpoche 46
peace (*she wa*) 14, 22-24, 37-38, 49, 77, 79-80, 90, 94
placement meditation 73, 92-93
prajña 47-48, 64, 66
preliminary practices 82-83
protectors, dharma 74,
reincarnation 33-36
relative level 12, 53-54
sadhānas 80
Sakya Paṇḍita 18
samādhi 102
saṃsāra see conditioned existence
saṅgha 26, 81-82
secret mantra 73
self/nonself 21-22, 25, 29-30, 35, 51
skandhas see aggregates.
skillful means 73, 77
spiritual powers 74, 76
spiritual song 94, 104-105
subtle channels 72
suffering 14-16, 25, 28
sūtra teachings 71-73, 68, 96, 103
tantra teachings 68, 71-73
three jewels 26

Tibetan Buddhism 11
torma offerings 81
two truths 13
Uttara Tantra 5-62,
unvirtuous actions 17-21, 39-40
vajra 71, 73
Vajradhara 87
Vinaya 38
vows 39-40
weariness of saṃsāra 100
wheel of dharma 13, 41, 50, 57
yidam 74, 76-81,